POWER TOOLS FOR POWER KIDS

By Birgit Baader

Dreamspace Publishing

Copyright © 2017 by Birgit Baader

All rights reserved.

Included in the New Zealand National Bibliography (NZNB): title – *Power Tools for Power Kids*, author – *Birgit Baader*

ISBN 13: 978-0-473-41670-6

CONTENTS

INTRODUCTION 1
    About this book 2
    For you… 10
    Playing with Fire 14
I AM, AM I? 17
    I am, am I? 18
    A basic map for Agents of the Impossible 19
    Your Inner Team 23
    Unpack your bag 25
    I am the creator of my world 30
    Finding your rhythm 36
    Monkey Mind 40
    Magic Mansion 46
    Journey into your Heart 51
    Your Dream-Self 53
    Crossing the Threshold 57
PRACTISING MAGIC 63
    Code of practise 64
    Power ABC 74
        Rituals & Ceremonies 76
        Set your intention 100
        Meet your Support Team in Spirit World 106
        Building new pathways – Cycles 112
        Power Codes & Magic Spells 118

Cleansing & clearing energies 128
Protection 136
Power Tools for every day 142
Letting go I 143
Letting go II – Riding wild horses 145
Your Magic Power Place 149
Talking with the Rock Family 152
Crystal Magic 158
Breathing with the River 170
Diamond Power Station 173
Super Powers 176
Beyond words – reading energy fields 180
Telepathy 187
Read my mind 194
Shapeshifting 200
The Art of Disappearing 209
Transfiguration 215
Teleportation 220
Trance – portal to the Otherworld 227
The Art of Dreaming 243
MAGIC LIFE ART 251
Magic Life Art 252
Earth Mandalas 253
Make your own Trance instrument 257
Altar – creating a sacred space 271
Power Pouch 277

Reading energy – make your own pendulum 280
Magic Wand 289
Playing with Fire 293
Make your own Smudging Set 305
Magic Potions 313
Build your own Medicine Wheel 325
Weaving Magic 345
Show your true colours 358
Dreamspace Art 360
Your Act of Power 364
USEFUL RESOURCES 369
Appendix 370
Links 374
Books 376
ACKNOWLEDGEMENTS 377
ABOUT THE AUTHOR 379
OTHER TITLES BY BIRGIT BAADER 380
CONNECT WITH BIRGIT 383

INTRODUCTION

About this book

A foreword for parents, caregivers, teachers, therapists ... (Dear young ones: you can read it, but might not need it)

I wrote this book to share old wisdom and techniques to restore the balance: when we find balance within ourselves it affects the balance of all Life. The Power Tools in this book support children to sculpture their full potential and to establish life-sustaining habits that will help them throughout their whole life. With these tools in their toolbox children will feel confident and safe. They will be able to navigate through life with more ease and trust, and always have something to come back to when they feel challenged, are at a turning point or look for orientation. They will learn to explore powerful elemental and universal tools that will connect them to the essence of Life and give them a deep sense of inner calm, guidance and reassurance.

The activities in this book incorporate basic principles and natural laws of "Life Magic". Some are based on shamanic techniques and indigenous traditions from all over the world. In indigenous cultures children and young people traditionally are prepared for life through various challenges and teachings to ensure not only their intellectual and physical, but also their emotional, spiritual and mental strength and balance are developed and nurtured. When my children where little, I looked for something in modern European culture that would hold

INTRODUCTION

the same values and help my children to grow into well-balanced adults. I wanted to give them something they could use when surfing the waves of life, something to assist them and empower them and give them orientation when they would feel insecure and in times of (inner and outer) chaos. I didn't find much that addressed deep questions and Life issues in an accessible way for young ones. It was completely missing in Western mainstream education and parenting.

I found that in our culture, some children are called "dysfunctional" or labeled with "pathogenic issues" (ADHD, Autism, Dyslexia, Hypersensitivity, etc.). There are therapy and treatment options that sometimes include elements of what I was looking for. However, I didn't find anything in mainstream education. I think it is important to make these valuable tools available – once again – for all (children). We all need them to live a well-balanced and sustainable life.

The Power Tools in this book involve the use of the right side of our brain. They stimulate innate knowing within your children and hold a space for it to develop and grow. They are fun and playful, and at the same time trigger something deep within that otherwise is suppressed or stays dormant in a lot of people when they grow up in modern society.

We all are more or less visibly affected by the living conditions we humans have created on this planet. Due to human activity the balance on this planet is shifting rapidly – our children feel this intuitively and a lot of them show "signs of concern and distress". They don't function that well anymore in "old systems": they show all sorts of symptoms that tell us that something is out of balance. A lot of young ones feel helpless and frustrated and are looking for ways to be and to express their confusion.

The tools in this book are examples that I have used to assist my own children and others on their path into adulthood. Tools to build a platform of habits and skills from which they can face life's challenges. Tools to help them answer their questions, to help them deal with their doubts and worries, to empower them to "dig deep" and to find that center of power within themselves. Tools to keep them connected to their inner wisdom and spiritual guidance. Tools to help them to expand their consciousness, to find new ways of being and to turn the wheel towards a sustainable lifestyle. And last but not least tools that help them to cope with the "adult world" around them and the unsustainable and not life-supportive systems they are often exposed to.

Some of the tools (or similar ones) have been in use since ancient times and are still used today, often by indigenous people. They have been neglected in mainstream Western societies where the focus was and still is more on the physical material world. The unseen realms of pure energy have been "on the back burner" for a long while. However, including them in the picture of our lives enables us to link into "the bigger picture" and underlying universal energies. It gives us a deeper understanding and awareness.

I drew inspiration from shamanic traditions, religions such as Buddhism, Hinduism, Christianity and followed my own intuition. Please feel free to adapt and play around with the Power Tools in this book and follow your inner guidance to create your own versions.

What do you get out of this book?

Tools are usually here to help us achieve something with more ease and efficiency. This is also true for the Power Tools in this book. The activities and rituals are designed to empower children and to ease their paths. By learning how to use these Power Tools they gain valuable skills that can serve them throughout their whole life. They will learn new "languages" to communicate and to relate in this world, tools to build sustainable systems and ways of being, tools to maintain their balance and wellbeing.

The Power Tools will empower (not only) children to

- balance themselves when they are upset, challenged, bored, hurt, sad, angry, restless, fearful, worried, unhappy, unwell
- listen to their intuition and receive guidance "from within"
- focus and concentrate their energies

- draw strength and inspiration from within themselves
- gain emotional, mental and physical balance
- be self-confident
- cope better with life's challenges
- improve relationship and social skills
- be proactive and express themselves in their own unique way
- access their power center from which creativity and self-management arise

The Power Tools help in situations of stress, frustration, disorientation, at turning-points and when facing challenges: friendship/relationship issues, family conflicts, school-related issues (e.g. academic achievement pressure, exams), grief, illness, traumatic experiences. I have used some of the tools with refugee children, and they helped them to regain their inner balance and to find new direction, hope and guidance from within.

The children will learn how to surf the waves of their energies without being "swept away". Imagine a lake or an ocean in a storm. The churning water, the waves and the spray make it impossible to see to the bottom. In tumultuous water we cannot see the ground. The surface has to be undisturbed and still, the high waves have to calm down, the wind has to cease. The Power Tools help

INTRODUCTION

children to establish a sound connection with themselves, so that they are able to reach a state of stillness where they can see to the bottom of things and find "peace of mind and heart". They empower them to build and access a stable platform from which they can live their lives in a harmonious way and reach their true potential.

How to use this book?

This book addresses YOU, young readers, directly. If you are an adult companion (parent, educator, caregiver, therapist, etc.) working with this book, the you-format supports you to address the children directly. For people who are too young or not able to read on their own yet, an older companion might be needed to choose the relevant Power Tools and adapt them accordingly. To ease the way there are age recommendations for each tool. They are, of course, just a suggestion and can be adapted to your needs and your (child's) abilities.

You will also find symbols at the beginning of each chapter to give you an indication of the level of care that is needed to use the tool (please also see *Playing with Fire*):

> age 5+

Green = all good, no worries – just play around and experiment with this Power Tool

age 5+

Yellow = be aware, follow your intuition

age 5+

Blue = attention, this might stir up some stuff, look for a trustworthy being that is there for you if needed

age 5+

Red = guidance needed, handle with care

Great in a group and/or together with an adult companion

Handle with care, get assistance – potentially harmful

Here is a brief overview of the different sections in this book:

Section 1 *I am, am I?* Contains a series of useful exercises and Tools that prepare you to live a magical, balanced and powerful life.

INTRODUCTION

Section 2, *Practice Magic*, is divided into three sub-categories: *Power ABC* contains the basics of practicing Magic, *Power Tools for every day* gives you some effective and practical Power Tools to get started (a bit like the time tables in Maths), and *Super Powers* introduces you to the next level of developing your magical skills.

It makes sense to read through the introductory chapters of section 2 *Practice Magic* to learn about the basics of Magic before you use certain Power Tools. However, I encourage you to use this book and its magic intuitively: Follow your inner guidance right from the beginning and trust that whatever attracts your attention will be "the right thing" for you to read.

Section 3, *Magic Life Art*, gives you the opportunity to create magic through crafts and by using your hands.

And in section 4, *Useful Resources*, you will find, well, exactly what the title says: useful resources to help you on your journey.

For you...

"In this lifetime we are like Superman who must remain disguised as the nerdy newspaper journalist Clark Kent, or Harry Potter and his friends who are not allowed to do magic while they are on holiday, away from Hogwarts School of Witchcraft and Wizardry... but even Harry Potter and Clark Kent get to tap into their 'special powers' once in a while, especially when the going gets tough."

Anthon St. Maarten

This book contains a set of basic Power Tools to help you hone some skills that keep you in touch with the world of magic, dreams and transformation. We are all born connected to these worlds. However, like we need to learn how to walk and talk with our physical bodies, we need to develop our skills and abilities to enter unseen realms and tap into power sources as well.

INTRODUCTION

The Power Tools in this book will get you started on your journey. Hopefully your experiences with them will make you curious to explore your own magic potential a bit more in depth as you grow and live your life. The tools will assist you to consciously tap into your power resources and to use your innate forces wisely and for the benefit of all Life. They certainly have made my life and the lives of many others I have learned from or shared these tools with a lot easier.

Choose what you love and what attracts your interest

Some of the Power Tools might already seem familiar to you, you might have heard of them, or seen others use them – or not. Follow your intuition and choose the tools that attract your interest. There is no need to pick up a carving knife, if carving doesn't interest you in the least. Chances are that you will never become a really amazing carver no matter how hard you practise. You might become technically skilled, but your creations most likely wouldn't be as inspired and awesome as they would be if carving actually was one of your passions.

Be patient and allow time to play around and explore

Once you found a Power Tool that you feel drawn to, be patient and allow time to explore its depths. Almost everything you learn in this lifetime takes a bit of perseverance: you have to allow time and hold a space for learning, and you have to give your energy and focus to the task, if you want to get anywhere with it. As a toddler we learn to speak over a period of 2-4 years (!), usually by being totally immersed in our mother tongue 24/7. Keep that in mind, when you learn anything new in your life. Most likely you won't use the Power Tools in this book 24/7, and it's unlikely that you live in an environment where people use them that often (if you do, then you probably won't need this book!).

Find your own style

Tools, in general, are here to help us: it's entirely up to us what we do with them. You can find your own style and experiment with various ways of using them. As with all tools: the more you get used to them, the more you practice, the more you can create with them, and the more amazing your "works" and outcome will be.

INTRODUCTION

As you get more adept with these basic Power Tools, you might want to explore further and find more "expert tools" to develop your skills. I am sure that you can put what you have learned in this book into good practice in order to attract more resources, human and non-human teachers into your life and to find inner guidance of how to plunge deeper into the realms of universal consciousness and Life Energy Magic. Beam your questions, dreams and wishes "out there" – and you will receive answers and messages using your Power Tools and special communication "devices" from this book.

I wish you a great journey and a lot of fun!

"Magic has a lot to do with telling yourself the truth about the way things are. It doesn't matter who else you tell it to."

Carol O'Biso

Playing with Fire

A note of caution

Power tools are – literally – powerful which means: they have to be handled with care if you don't want to hurt yourself or others. If you buy a chainsaw, it is wise to read the instruction manual and start slowly by getting some skills under your belt before you go into the woods. A simple hammer can be used both in a constructive and destructive way. When lighting a fire, it is good to know about its qualities and powers in order to make sure that you are safe: A fire can give you warmth and cook your food, but you can also burn yourself or it can burn down your house.

At first glance, most Power Tools in this book aren't as dangerous as a chainsaw or a blazing fire. However, they are powerful tools that are able to change realities and affect how you perceive your life. So please be aware and handle them with care. Set a clear and life-supportive intention and use them to the benefit of all Life, not to increase your own power over others, to control or to dominate.

Some "health & safety" guidelines

As a general rule, trust your intuition and trust yourself: If it doesn't feel "right", don't do it.

Don't force yourself! (Children usually don't need this advice – they naturally feel drawn to what's good/right for them at any given moment.) The Power Tools can be most helpful when there is resonance deep within you. If a Tool/activity doesn't resonate with you, don't use it ☺

Follow the guidelines outlined at the beginning of some of the activities. They are there to help you and to keep you safe. Some of the tools originate from shamanic traditions and can lead you into other realities. Hence, it is important to anchor and ground yourself to be able to safely "travel between the worlds".

When you see this sign...

... please pay special attention to how you use this tool. Don't play tricks on others or scare them on purpose. Don't use it to brag or to exert power over others. If you disregard this advice you might not only harm others, but also your Self at the same time.

The symbols below the title will give you an indication about the recommended level of care and the suitable age range. Please note that these are only guidelines based on my experiences and observations.

Have fun! Be playful! And most importantly: trust your intuition.

Most young children do that "by default". Older children might need to re-adjust, but will quickly learn as these factors are natural drivers and innate to us all.

I wish you great fun rekindling the fire of your own power, tending the fire, playing with fire, using the power of fire to your own benefit and to the benefit of all life.

I AM, AM I?

I am, am I?

Do you sometimes want to know who you really are? Do you ask yourself: What am I doing here? Where do I come from and where do I go?

In this section we will explore these questions. You might get a clearer picture of how to find answers along the way. You will get some tools for guidance, some tools to create the life you want, some tools to support you to feel happy and well.

Use them as often as you like. As with any tool, you will become more and more adept the more you use it and the results will be more and more sophisticated and refined over time.

Pack your own tool box: There might be tools that you feel more drawn to than others – just test and explore them and use them as you see fit. And, most importantly: Have fun with the Power Tools. They are here to help you to discover who you are and to support you in challenging times – not another thing to add to your to-do-list.

A basic map for Agents of the Impossible

In this book you will find many pointers and tools that will support and empower you. It's all about how to find balance, to (re-) claim your power and to make you a strong and cheerful Agent of the Impossible. Here is a very basic map that you can use as an overall guide to navigate joyfully and confidently through your life – especially when the going gets tough.

You have a unique songline that stays with you throughout your whole life. You can write different stories or verses in your life, but you cannot change your unique songline or Life Tone. Finding out your songline is like finding the red thread in your life: you will get an idea where you are heading – which is of great help when you feel lost or have questions like "what's the point", "where am I going", "what am I here for", etc.

You might already know your songline and know, deep inside, what really matters to you, what you want to explore and spend your energies on in this lifetime. That's great – keep coming back to it! Keep singing that song, keep it alive within you, so that you can always hear it – even when there is a lot of noise around you or others try to sing over you.

If you don't know or aren't sure about your songline, that's fine, too. It's there! You only need to become aware of it. How can you do this? Bring your attention from the outside to the inside: stop, be still, find that place of stillness within your Self, breathe and listen... It may take some time – depending on how noisy and crazy your mind will go –, but you will hear it... eventually!

Tips:

Your song is loudest when you feel happy, full of joy, in balance.

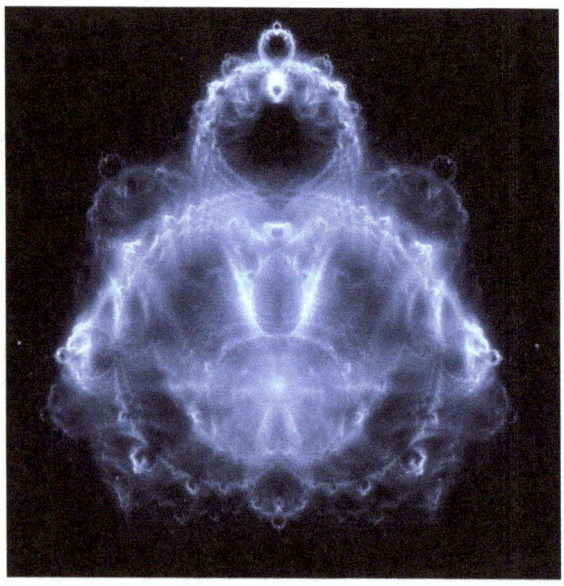

Here are a few more pointers to support you on your journey:

Stick to your song

Your song is your guideline, your compass that leads the way and makes sure that you stay "on track". So it is important that you take time to listen and that you keep true to your songline. Why? Whenever you don't follow your song, you feel lost, unhappy, stuck, angry, desperate, depressed, frustrated, confused, disoriented, exhausted. Your song will lead you through many life experiences – not all may be pleasant and easy, but all will add to your knowledge and wisdom and power and help you to explore the terrains that you set out to explore. Learn to listen to your song, commit to it and you will have a clear beacon that guides you throughout your life.

Align your Self with Life Energy

Life moves in cycles. After each night a new day begins. And the day transitions into the next night. Spring follows winter and leads into summer, then into autumn before a new cycle around the sun begins – year after year after year. There are countless other examples. Be aware of the cycles in your life. Recognize the beginnings and the endings. See how they affect your life, your relationships. There always are beginnings and endings, and new beginnings and new endings... To know this, to accept it and go with the flow of Life will ease your path immensely.

Find out more in *Building new pathways* and *Medicine Wheel*.

Take care of your vessel(s)

On our way through life we choose many vessels, instruments and forms to express our song and to write our life's stories. An important one, for instance, is our physical body. Any tool, vessel or vehicle work best when it is well maintained and taken care of. And: ideally, it is serviced regularly, on an ongoing basis. Imagine that you only had a shower to clean your body at the beginning of the year. Or imagine you'd wash the dishes only once a month. Well, to keep things in good working condition most of us have to do it all the time, right? Cleaning, cleansing, purifying is always necessary to keep things in a good flow, so we better accept "maintenance" as a vital part of Life – and learn to enjoy it and to make it fun.

Some important maintenance areas that need our constant attention to assure a smooth journey are: our **physical vessel** (body), our **mental vessel** (mind/ thoughts/ beliefs), our **spiritual vessel** (soul/connection channels to the unseen world/Dreamspace, to magic and non-human realms).

In this book you will find a few maintenance tools to make sure that your three main vessels are fully functioning and in good condition.

Your Inner Team

age 5+

Have you noticed that you sometimes seem to be "different people", all in one body? There are Happy-Chappy, Funny-Bunny, there might also be Grumpy-Bumpy, Silly-Billy, Sad- (or Mad-) Face... and probably quite a few others. It can be very valuable to know all these different guys inside of you. I call them my inner team. There are the Dreamer, the Dancer, the Teacher, the Learner, the Organiser, the Networker, the Friend, the Pleaser, the Teaser, the Shy-one, the Fighter, the Self-Righteous one... As you can see, there are quite a few actually, and it took me a while to get to know them all and to find out their needs and wants. I realised that they all want my best and that they are all here to help me. Yes, Grumpy-Bumpy and Mad-Face as well. They usually step in when I did not listen to Nurturer or Carer, the ones who make sure I get enough rest and care well for my Self. Or when somebody oversteps my boundaries.

Your inner team is always there for you to help you find balance in your life and to make decisions and choices that will support you in the long run.

1. Make a list or draw pictures of your inner team.
2. Observe your Self and notice when different team members show up. What triggers them? When do they step in? Find out what roles they play.

3. What messages do they have for you? What do they bring "to the table"? Listen to their different voices and explore what they want to tell you.

4. Like in any team, every single team member has unique qualities and skills. You are the coach of your team. A good coach might sometimes need to "reign in" a talented midfield player who never passes to his/her team mates because he or she thinks they can win the game on their own. Get to know your team members and their unique skills, their strengths and their weaknesses. Learn when you need to reign them in and how to best use their strengths. Stay open to what they have to say – and consider their messages when making decisions in your life.

   For example: Your "Friend" might want to go to a party while your "Nurturer/Carer" might tell you it is better to stay home and have some quiet time. As a good coach you will consider both voices and make a decision that is best for the whole team (= your Self) in the long run.

5. Find out which team members collaborate and which ones are in conflict. This will help you to manage your team like a good coach and to navigate through situations of inner turmoil and confusion.

6. Be gentle with your Self if different team members "play up" and cause trouble. Listen to them all and make your decision based on what serves you best in the long run and from an overall perspective.

Unpack your bag

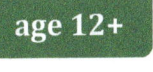

Do you sometimes feel overwhelmed? Weighed down by expectations, tasks and emotions? Do you feel like you can "never be good enough"? I think we all feel like this from time to time. It is usually a sign that we carry too much baggage! Baggage that others (or sometimes ourselves) have put into our bags and that doesn't belong to us: it hinders us and weighs us down. Here is a great tool to "clear the space" and get rid of all the "stuff" that you don't need.

As we grow up, people pass on or share things with us all the time. Those "things" can usually be sorted in five categories: knowledge, advice, skills, opinions, wisdom – in short: KASOW.

Here are some examples:

Knowledge: "The oven is hot when the red light is on." – "Mammals give birth to live babies."

Advice: "Don't touch the oven when it's hot." – "Learn how to read and write if you want to be successful in life."

Skills: reading, playing guitar, playing soccer, dancing

Opinions: "You are beautiful." – "You are useless at maths."

Wisdom: "Everything happens for a reason."

I am sure you can think of many other examples.

1. Take some time to reflect and think about the KASOWs you have been given so far in your life. *What baggage are you carrying around with you?*

   You can make notes to remember it all, if you want to.

2. Take a bag and find some objects that represent your KASOWs.

   Be spontaneous and playful and just grab what "shows up" in front of you: natural things like stones, pieces of wood, etc. or, if you are indoors, anything that you feel drawn to in your environment that represents a particular KASOW. If you want, you can label the objects (e.g. write on them or tag them with stickers – the second option may be a better idea if it's one of your mum's precious vases...).

   Take as much time as you want. Sometimes, you will find it easy to identify your KASOWs and your bag will be full before you know it. At other times, it might take a while to gather all the "goodies" that have been handed to you by others.

3. Once you feel you are finished for now and have compiled a few things, allow yourself some time to look at them.

Why have you chosen this particular object?

The answers to this question can reveal a lot and often show you the value that you link to a particular KASOW.

4. Look at all the objects and ask yourself three questions:
   1. *Is this useful for me, or not?*
   2. *Why is it useful for me (or why not)?*
   3. *What do I want to keep?*

   Follow your feeling with this last question and only keep what feels "right" and "good" and "easy/light"; after all, you want to end up with a nice and easy-to-carry bag, right?

5. Sort things out!

   Start with the objects that you do not want to keep: all the don'ts and do's that weigh you down and don't serve you well; all the opinions about you that are not really relevant to you, not supportive or that do not represent who you truly are or want to be; all the skills that might be great, but just not for you; all the well-meaning advice that might have helped others but simply doesn't ring true to you.

   Be as rigorous, as thorough, as careful as you need to be, and return the objects to where you took them from. Place them where they belong and farewell them: "Thank you for being with me for a while. I do no longer wish to carry you with me – be well."

Deal with the things you aren't sure next – if there are any. If you are not sure, whether you need it or not, whether it is good advice or not, then you might want to discard it! As said before: you want to end up with a light pack on your back, so only keep "stuff" that clearly feels important TO YOU. As above: when you are finished place the objects where they belong and farewell them. This is important as the physical action of bringing the objects back and bidding them farewell helps your mind to let go of the KASOW and to literally release the weight on your shoulders.

Now that you have come this far, you hopefully end up with some "goodies": knowledge and information that are relevant TO YOU; advice that makes sense TO YOU and helps you realise your dreams; skills that you are interested in, that are fun, that you love to acquire; opinions that are worth considering (be careful with opinions, though: they often lead to judgmental behaviour and prejudice – be sure to seriously question them before you take them on board); and wisdom that can guide you on your path.

Double-check if the remaining objects really serve you. Are they supporting you in all your aspects? Do they feel easy and light to carry (or do they burden you)? Do they lift your spirits, give you guidance and in general make you feel good? If so, great! You might choose to keep the objects that you collected as reminders (unless it is mum's precious vase – you have to give that one back, probably). If you feel like it, keep them in a special place or make a special bag for them (also see *Altar* and *Power Pouch*). If you don't want to keep them, thank them for being in your life and return them.

6. Check your bag from time to time! Especially, when you feel overwhelmed, weighed down, frustrated, depressed, stressed, disoriented. As we continue our journey through life, we always accumulate "new stuff". Each day someone shares KASOWs with us! So we have to keep unpacking and packing our bags again and again, asking ourselves continuously if there is something that doesn't serve us or something we'd like to add – much in the same way as we have to unpack our bag after each sleepover or holiday, getting the old clothes out, washing them or giving them away because they are too small or torn, getting rid of what we don't like, etc., and then pack our bag anew for the next part of our journey through Life.

I am the creator of my world

age 8+

Yes, you are! If this is "old news" to you – great. If not: this is a pretty powerful statement that can change how you approach the world. It means that, deep within yourself, you create everything, every situation that you experience. You are incredibly powerful and you can influence how you are affected by the things that happen within and around you!

If you apply this Power Tool, you can consciously create the experiences you want in your life – or, at the start, you will at least be able to influence your experiences and orientate yourself towards your "dream life".

Be aware: this Tool – like most powerful tools – needs to be handled with care. Everything you create and manifest comes with its own dynamic. This means, if you create uplifting things for yourself and others, this will raise the frequency within yourself and in your environment and create something "good". If you create "shit", it will smell badly, and the smell will affect yourself and others! So be careful what you wish for – it might backfire or smell bad ☺

I am the creator of my life.

That is kind of easy to accept with nice things, but what about not so nice things? What about a fight with your best friend? Trouble in school? Traumatic experiences (accidents, war, natural disasters), illness, poverty? Why on earth would you create that?

First of all, most people don't know that they are the creator of their life and therefore do not *consciously* create their experiences. They unconsciously and randomly create situations and experiences that enable them to learn certain lessons they came to learn. This can end up being quite unpleasant and messy at times.

Second, you are not the only one creating experiences! There are many others around you, and you'll be affected by their creations. Especially, if it's about "collective creations", learning experiences that affect a whole family, group, country, generation.

Third, we all create experiences in our life to learn something. Some choose "beginner" lessons, others commit to the advanced level that comes with huge challenges, others again choose to "revisit" a lesson that has been in their family/country/culture for generations and still needs to be learned. Before we are born we tune into a certain energetic frequency – it's like choosing a radio channel with music we want to listen to. The thing is: most of us are not aware that a) we can choose the channel we want to listen to, and b) that we were born tuned into a certain frequency.

I will give you an example: if you choose the 99.8 frequency on your radio, you will only be able to listen to the program of this particular radio station – and not to all the others that are available. At least not at the same time, and not unless they overwrite your chosen frequency. The experiences you create are your radio program: unless you change the frequency, you will only be listening to your chosen program.

Fourth, you might not always be able to change certain things that are thrown at you (for example: illness, conflict, accidents, death), but you are always in charge of how you deal with them. You can choose the program that you want to listen to, simply by tuning into a certain frequency.

Use the following Power Tool to consciously tune into a frequency you like. Once you are familiar with it, you can use it on your own as often as you like. When you first use it, you might want to get somebody to assist you and read out the steps (you can also record them). If nobody is around or can make time, you can do it while reading it to yourself.

1. Find a comfortable place where you will be undisturbed, turn off your phone, computer and other devices and put everything aside that could distract you.

2. Think about how you would like to feel or something you would really like to do or be within the next few weeks or months...

3. Next, imagine…

    … a sweet, juicy orange…

    … taste it in your mouth, on your tongue, between your teeth…

    Imagine now…

    … a spoonful of your favourite ice-cream…

    Feel how it melts in your mouth, taste its flavour…

    Imagine…

    … freshly baked bread…

    Smell it, still warm from the oven, and taste the first crunchy bite…

    Now taste the yummy feast you will have to celebrate once you have achieved what you want…

    Taste all your favourite foods…

    Imagine…

    … the sweet smell of a beautiful flower…

    … the smell of pine needles…

    … the delicious smell of a freshly baked cake…

    Now smell how it smells once you have achieved what you want…

    Gently touch the soft belly of a little puppy…

    Now wade through a tub of warm honey…

    Knead some bread dough with your wet hands…

Feel the warm sand under your feet...

And now feel how it feels once you have achieved what you want...

Hear the sound of a rainstorm on the roof...

Hear a drummer beating a steady rhythm...

Hear your favourite singer sing a song...

Now hear how it sounds once you have achieved what you want...

Imagine...

... the rising sun, coming up above the horizon...

... the fresh green leaves in spring time...

See a shooting star falling from the sky...

See a good friend's face looking at you...

And now see whatever you want to achieve being the way you want it to be. Feel it with all your senses and as detailed as you can imagine. See it accomplished; feel how happy/well/proud/pleased/relaxed you will feel. Dream it all up and enjoy it.

4. Take some deep breaths.
5. Then, go through all your senses again:

   taste it...

   touch it...

   smell it...

see it...

hear it...

feel it in every detail you can imagine...

Tip:

Do this as often as you like. By doing so, you tune into the frequency of your Dream Life with all your senses – consciously choosing the radio program you want to listen to!

Imagining in detail and with all your senses what you want to experience in life is an immensely powerful tool to consciously and deliberately create your reality.

Finding your rhythm

age 5+

You are who you are – enjoy it! Feel it! Show it!

We all have our own "groove" that defines how we live our life. To know yours is valuable, so that you can adjust your pace accordingly and don't overwhelm yourself or others. Imagine a big orchestra playing a symphony. There are many different instruments, playing different melody lines – and yet, they all sound beautiful together. They wouldn't if the clarinets all of a sudden would play the lines of the kettledrums.

If you know your rhythm, you can follow it and stick to it. And whenever you do that, you will feel strong and in balance. It sometimes happens that we are swept away by other people's rhythms – and all of a sudden we might realise that we feel frustrated, unhappy, uncomfortable. This usually happens when we are with people who play a completely different rhythm that doesn't go well together with ours. Sometimes, it is possible to adjust our rhythms so that we can play along nevertheless. At other times, it might be good to acknowledge that our rhythm simply doesn't fit with the one of another person.

You will feel when you are "at ease" and "in sync", when you feel in your power and supported and good. *Knowing* your rhythm enables you to recognise other people's rhythms and to *choose* how to play along – or not.

1. You need a drum or another rhythm instrument; preferably one that resonates nicely and has a sound you like. Of course, you can also use a few sticks, a spoon and a cooking pot or whatever else you like to bang on ☺

2. Find a comfortable space where you can be on your own for a bit.

3. Find a comfortable position (if possible with your back straight so that your energy can flow freely along your spine). When you are ready, start softly playing a rhythm. Simply begin... even if you feel unsure and don't know what to do. Let yourself go... the rhythm(s) will come by itself.

   Give yourself time. Just play and have fun.

   Amongst different rhythms that may come up, you will recognise your core rhythm: it will flow naturally from your hands, and you will feel good, strong and light while playing it.

Tips:

1. Once you know your own rhythm, you may want to start experimenting with different rhythms and volumes. Go wild: try to play louder, softer, weaker, stronger, faster, slower... and observe yourself.

   How do different rhythms make you feel?

2. Can you feel your heartbeat and drum along to it for a while?

Playing with others:

3. Before you play with others, whether with other people or other creatures or elements, it is important that you have found your own rhythm and know how it feels. Why? So that you can always come back to your own rhythm and won't lose yourself in other rhythms.

4. Lie on the ground and feel the heartbeat of Mother Earth – calm, steady, peaceful, powerful...

    You will feel it best, if you sit or lie directly on the ground outside, on a meadow or in the forest.

5. Play your drum outside, if you can. Feel the many different rhythms of Nature and try to play in sync with them.

6. Air, Water, Fire, Earth – they all have their own rhythms. It's fun to play together with them – try it.

7. Get to know other rhythms and learn to play them. Then practise to play your own rhythm together with other rhythms.

    When you play with several people, it may take a while before you all play together in harmony. Take your time. Observe how the sounds differ from each other. Some may be loud and dominant, others softer and tentative, some strong and rhythmical, others a bit wobbly and hesitant. Let your hands and your whole body find your own rhythm while listening to the others.

8. Your rhythm may also change over time: As said before, you can always recognise your core rhythm, because it flows easily and feels familiar and good.

Monkey Mind

age 8+

What is the mind?

Are you your mind?

Are you what you think you are? And are you who you think you are?

Philosophers, religious leaders and teachers, cognitive scientists, psychologists and many other individuals and groups of people have been trying to understand and to explain "the mind". And they still haven't come to a final conclusion ☺

In our language, "mind" often has the same meaning as "thoughts". The mind, however, is undoubtedly much more than that. Consciousness, memory, imagination, visualisation are all things the mind is involved in. I won't go into a detailed discussion here about what the mind actually is and about the different mind-boggling concepts that various thinkers and mind-researchers came up with. It looks like it is no easy task to understand the mind using the mind... You can make up your own mind about this and try answering the questions above. They are an interesting playing field for your Mind!

In this chapter I want to focus on why it is important to manage your Mind consciously. Your Mind is a powerful Tool. It can be super-helpful to weigh up the pros and the cons of something when making a decision, to make a step-by-step plan, or to collect facts and numbers to assess a certain topic. Your Mind, your thoughts, your imagination are your carving Tools to help you shape your life: you create your physical reality with them. They are sharp – and if you don't pay attention, they cut wildly through your brain jungle (also see *Building new pathways*) and shape your actions in a way that might not always be what you want or what serves you well. When your Mind is jumping from one thing to another, it can make you nervous, restless and unfocused. It might keep you awake at night, not let you rest or concentrate on your game or project. Like a horde of wild monkeys, your Mind, your thoughts and beliefs can leave a lot of damage behind.

This is why a lot of wisdom teachers came up with various techniques "to control" the Mind. As control for me often evokes the image of force, I prefer to use the word "to manage". Be *mind*ful and get a grip on your Mind-Tool. Use its sharp edges and powerful qualities with awareness so that you can consciously shape your life.

Observing wild monkeys

Have you ever wanted to observe animals in the wild? Now you have the opportunity to be an explorer and do some interesting and fun research. But be aware, the research object is wild, at times, very elusive and not easy to grasp: your Mind, your thoughts and beliefs. You have to be still and sit patiently in the bushes, waiting and observing what happens...

Try to watch your thoughts like a movie: *What images does your Mind conjure up?*

What are you thinking about your Self? About others? About the world?

What thoughts cross your Mind when something triggers you?

You probably will soon notice that it is a bit like catching rain drops – or wild monkeys for that matter. There is a constant flow of thoughts. They don't come in a predictable order, and you never know where and when they will pop up next.

It doesn't matter! Let them be. You don't have to catch them. Just *observe* them.

Observe your thoughts and watch them come up and ebb away like waves in the ocean.

Tips:

1. I usually find it easiest to watch my thoughts and the images in my head while I close my eyes and sit or lie comfortably at a place where I won't be interrupted or distracted by others.

2. Pay attention to your feelings.

   At times, you may pick up thoughts and images in your head that make you feel really good. You might think of a moment when you were hanging out with a close friend, or remember the feeling of the soft fur of your dog friend under your hands. At other times, you might have thoughts and images that make you feel not so good: sad, angry, worried, restless, frustrated...

Let everything come up and let it be.

3. Learn to discern thoughts that make you feel good and thoughts that don't.

Find out which monkeys do a lot of damage in the jungle and which ones are fun to watch and lift your energy.

What are they doing? How do they make you feel?

If you want to can write them down in a journal:

Thinking of ... makes me feel sad.

Thinking of ... makes me feel happy.

4. Be the Monkey Master.

Once you know your horde of monkeys quite well and are able to notice which ones make you feel good and which ones not, you can continue to the next important step: leave your observer's position and step into the horde of wild monkeys! Pick the ones that do a lot of harm (= don't make you feel good) and stop them.

How to do that?

Here is one simple way of doing it: Let's pick the "nobody likes me/I am not likeable"-monkey that might be raging through your thought-jungle sometimes (or choose any other monkey that makes you feel uncomfortable). Whenever you see him pop up in the branches within your head, take a deep breath and gather your Super Powers. Imagine that you have a Super Power that can freeze things. Direct that Super Power towards the monkey-thought and freeze it. It will stop it in its tracks immediately.

Take another deep breath and direct your attention towards a monkey that makes you feel good (you can also direct your attention to your one-word intent, see chapter *Set your intention*). Breathe and deliberately focus on your feel-good monkey.

If your trouble-causing monkey stirs up again, take another deep breath and sent him another dose of your Freeze Super Power. Some monkey thoughts and images are pretty strong and persistent, so you might have to repeat the process several times.

With the help of your breath and your Super Powers, you will be able to manage your horde of wild monkeys. You will learn to stop the "troublemakers" right at the start, when they show up. They will, over time, calm down and settle or simply disappear into the jungle. And, as a consequence, "good vibes" will spread in your jungle: the more you concentrate on the cool monkeys (the ones that create a good vibe and atmosphere), the more their energy will spread and rub off on the others. One by one, you will fill your mind-jungle with calm and positive stuff – and your monkey-thoughts will become your support crew helping you to bring into your life whatever you want.

"What you focus on is what you hold in your consciousness. And so that is how you feel, and that is how you are."

George Harrison (The Beatles)

Magic Mansion

age 5+

When you were born, you came with a lot of Powers, boxes full of them actually. You moved into your new body-house and tried to settle in. There was a lot to learn. You needed to figure out how to use your new environment, for example how to move around, how to maintain it with food and drinks... It was quite a journey to figure out the basics and get used to this rather dense and bulky thing called body.

While settling in, some get so used to the body-house that they think they are the body-house and it is all there is. They forget that they are wizards and magicians that can roam the Universe freely. And that they can dream and conjure up things as they wish. Some take their body-house for granted: they forget to look after it, to check the rooms regularly and see if there is any cleaning or maintenance to do.

It is good to remind yourself that your body is like your house: you live in it for a while. It is your house. It belongs to you, but it is not your Self. If you take good care of it, it will be a nice cozy place that provides shelter and a safe platform from where to create your Life Magic.

Here are some basic Housekeeping Tools for your Magic Mansion. They will help you to be healthy, confident and strong within your body.

Tool 1

This is a good Tool to start with and to get used to check in with your body whenever you want to.

1. Close your eyes. Visualise your left hand.

   See and feel the bones in your hand, your fingers...

   Feel the cells of your skin...

   Feel and "see" your hand in as much detail as you can.

Tip:

When you begin using this Tool, it might help you to touch your hand and to gently caress it. Then take the other hand away and feel the sensation left behind.

2. Feel the connection that you have with your hand. Your hand is part of your Magic Mansion... every little cell of it is a building block of your Magic Mansion...

3. Move your hand a little, stretch and bend your fingers...

   Feel the many things that work together to make this possible...

Tip:

If your body doesn't allow you to move (for example if you are living in a paralysed body), you can still use this Tool and simply visualise your hand and fingers move...

Tool 2

Once you have mastered Tool 1, you might want to experiment with this upgraded version.

1. Make yourself comfortable and close your eyes.
2. Go through an imaginary journey through your body. It doesn't matter where you start. Start somewhere and from there, visit your whole body: go along your bones, through your veins, into your organs... your stomach, your liver, your kidneys, your intestines, your lungs, your heart ... Go visit your brain and all its various parts, and say hello to your throat on the way...
3. Wherever you go, smile and say "thank you" and feel grateful for what your Magic Mansion gives you.
4. On your journey, you might come to a place in your body that feels "odd", tense or not well. Stay there for a while and ask whether there is anything you can do to make it better.

The more you go on these journeys through your body, the easier you will pick up its messages and feel what to do. You will be able to spot the things that need your attention. It might be just a cleanse or some rest. It might be something else. Trust that you will feel what's needed.

If you do this often, you will establish a close connection to your body-house. This will help you to keep your Magic Mansion tidy, well functioning and comfortable to live in.

Tool 3

This is an extension of Tool 1 and 2. I find it useful in various situations, and it will also prepare you to use some of the other Tools described later in this book.

1. Close you eyes.
2. Choose a body part, for example your hand or foot. Connect with this body part (see Tool 1).
3. Breathe deeply, and with each out-breath feel how it becomes warmer and warmer... Feel the heat spread...

   Focus on this for 1-2 minutes.
4. You can move to other body parts if you want to, until your whole body feels warm. By the way: This is a basic version of a Tool that Tibetan monks use to increase their body temperature so that they can sit outside in icy conditions and not freeze to death.

Tip:

If you use Tool 3 regularly, you will eventually be able to evoke the desired result in your body within seconds. You can experiment with other outcomes as well. I often use it to heal or balance myself: I visualise, for instance, how the skin cells on my finger merge together and heal a cut. With a bit of practise you will be able to balance colds, sore throats and even more serious illnesses.

The great thing: if you use Tool 2 regularly, you will be able to detect and balance any illnesses long before they occur. It's like house-keeping: if you clean and tidy up on a regular basis, things are kept in good shape and will last longer.

Journey into your Heart

age 5+

This Power Tool will help you to balance yourself and be well when things around you are a bit stormy and wild, and whenever you want to focus and center yourself.

Until you are familiar with it, it might be easiest if you have somebody guiding you through the "steps". You can also read and record the whole sequence and adapt it to your own needs. Allow time for each step – the longer the breaks, the more time and space you have to explore (the "..." indicate where you might want to include some longer breaks).

I recommend that you close your eyes. Humans are very much relying on their visual sense, therefore some people feel a bit uncomfortable and reluctant to close their eyes. However, closing our eyes has many benefits. When you close your eyes your other senses become much more alert: blind people have much better hearing skills, for instance, and their sense of touch, the ability to feel the presence of someone, etc. is much more developed. If you close your eyes, you will train your ability to be fully present and your ability to perceive your environment with your other senses. You also won't be distracted so much by what you see in your surroundings which allows you to focus on your Self and other ways of knowing.

The more you use this Power Tool, the more you will develop the skill to pre-sense what's happening within and around you. It will help you to feel calm and centered.

1. Find a spot where you are comfortable and undisturbed for a while.
2. Take a few deep breaths... and close your eyes...
3. Listen to the sounds around you...

   Start with the sounds that are far, far away...
4. Breathe deeply...

   Now guide your attention to the sounds that are a bit closer to you...
5. Breathe deeply...

   Now focus on sounds that are in your close proximity...
6. Breathe deeply...

   Listen to the sounds of your body...

   In your ears...

   ...your breathing...

   ...your heart...
7. Feel your heart...

   Your heart keeps your body alive...

   Feel the gratitude that it keeps your body alive...
8. Breathe deeply into your heart...

   And when you are ready open your eyes and come back to the "outside world".

Your Dream-Self

age 8+

You can be anything you want to be!

Don't let external factors stop you. I have met people in wheelchairs who run marathons, I have interviewed a blind young man who is a free climber and climbs where a lot of his mates with normal vision wouldn't climb. There are other examples. How do these people do it "against all odds"?

First, they stick to their dream no matter what. They do not allow their environment (people around them, the location where they grow up, circumstances they live in), their physical condition (anything that has to do with their body: shape, handicaps, illness), or any other adverse or challenging circumstances to distract them from their dream.

Second, they have a "can-do" attitude, and follow their dream with determination. Even if your circumstances seem less than ideal to realise your dream, keep dreaming, keep visualising, keep holding it within you. When you doubt you can ever reach it, how do you deal with those doubts? Trust me, all of us know self-doubt, even the people I mentioned above. The difference is how we deal with our doubts. Do we allow them to stop us, or are we able to gently but firmly put them in their place?

Third, they persevere. They keep going, they keep dreaming, they don't deviate. They follow the road towards their dream, no matter how long, stony or challenging it might be. They accept mistakes, set-backs, "failures" as part of the journey and keep their dreams alive no matter what.

Fourth, they enjoy. They have fun! When they dream about what they want to be, what they want to achieve, what they want to experience, this "vision" gives them pleasure. And you probably know from your own experience: if you love something, it will keep you motivated. It makes all the efforts "worth it". A ballet dancer will persevere and keep practising difficult choreographies and postures, because he loves to move his body to the music; a musician will play her instrument until her fingers move fast enough to play the most intricate melodies.

The following Power Tool will help you to stay focused on your way towards your Dream Self: create something that represents how you want to be, how you want to feel. It can be anything!

1. Look for a place where you will be at peace and undisturbed for a while.

   A place where you feel safe and comfortable. Natural places can support you and help you to "see the bigger picture". If you live in a city and have no access to a garden or a park, it can be anywhere where you can retreat and be on your own for a bit.

2. Breathe and just allow yourself to be.

    You don't have to do anything. Let everything flow. If there is "stuff" that worries or bugs you, let it flow out of your sphere while breathing out. If you are close to a river, breathe it into the river and let it be washed away. You can also just visualise water flowing through you and taking everything away that makes you tense – like an internal shower that cleanses and releases everything that needs to go. Do this until you feel calm and relaxed.

3. Imagine your Dream-Self.

    How do you want to be? How do you want to feel?

    Go into every detail: see it, hear it, feel it, even taste it. The more senses you involve the better. My Dream-Self tastes like freshwater and juicy strawberries... Daydream your Self in as much detail as you want. Enjoy your Self ☺

4. Time to play and be creative!

    Do you have a favourite art form to express yourself in an artistic way? Do you like to draw, to dance, to sing, to carve, to write, to make music, to weave, to perform? Whatever form you choose, let yourself run free and enjoy the process of creating something that reminds you of your Dream-Self.

    If you aren't drawn to any particular art form, you could do a collage, either on paper or with a collection of objects: find images, materials, objects, anything that reminds you of your Dream-Self.

Don't be too serious – things might "pop up" when you least expect it.

Take your time.

Enjoy!

Dream of yourself and see what shows up.

Create something that represents your Dream-Self. If you choose to perform your Dream-Self, you can film or record it, to have something to "come back to" in the future.

Allow yourself as much time as you need! It may take 5 minutes, 5 days, 5 weeks, months, years ... time doesn't matter. Important is that you do it – thus linking in with your Dream-Self.

5. Once you have finished the creation of your Dream-Self reminder, place it somewhere where you can see it regularly. Every time you look at it, it will trigger the feeling and vision of your Dream-Self and will help you to realise it. You can also sit with it and ask questions if you like: your Dream-Self holds your energy and is able to give you directions when you need them.

Tip:

Do steps 1-3 as often as you can and like. It's a fun and extremely powerful Tool, in order to realise your dreams.

Crossing the Threshold

age 12+

This is a very powerful Tool and you need to learn how to use it wisely. It might be a bit of a challenge, and you might need to push your boundaries, but the results are extremely rewarding. Like with any tool: the more powerful it is, the more difficult to handle and the greater its outcome and effect.

This Power Tool will enable you to read signs and symbols of who you truly are reflected in Nature. It will help you to access other realms where you get answers to your questions, find guidance and orientation, solutions, peace of mind and heart, and much more. It will let you feel your close connection to Nature, and show you how to allow Nature to be your teacher and guide. Like all the other Tools it can be a hugely valuable Tool throughout your whole life.

Before you use this Tool, let somebody know about your plans! Why? Because it is always wise to let another person know where you are, if you "disappear" for a while. You might trip over a stone, twist your ankle and need help. Others might look for you, and worry where you are, etc. Tell your parents, grandparents, aunties, caregiver, anybody you trust what you are going to do and when/where.

This Tool comes with several "power levels": on level 1, you go for about 1 hour. Level 2 will be for 3 hours. Level 3 for 6 hours, and level 4 from dawn to dusk. All levels might hold different challenges for you – be gentle with yourself. Just make sure that you find a safe spot, and you will be fine.

1. Choose a place in Nature where you will be alone, ideally as far away as possible from the normal hustling and bustling of human beings and their buildings.

   Depending on where you live this can be a bit challenging. If you don't have a jungle right next door, no secluded park close-by and no rampant garden with magic hidden corners, you might want to ask somebody if they can drive you to a place like that. It can also be wise to double-check with an adult you trust if the place of your choice is a safe place for you to be.

2. Choose the power level you want to play at, and prepare yourself for your adventure.

   To fully embrace the experience, don't take anything to eat, only water to drink. In many cultures around the world, young women and men have ceremonies where they spend a certain length of time in Nature, fasting, to help them with significant transitions in their life.

If you want, take a small backpack with a water bottle, First Aid kit, blanket, a tube of honey (to boost your energy in case something happens, for example in case you twist an ankle), especially if you play at the higher levels and/or if you go to a very remote place.

3. Once you have chosen a place and time and the level you want to play, you are ready to start your journey!

   When you arrive at the place, create a simple ceremony: build a threshold with materials that you find in your surroundings – stones, leaves, sticks, grass... The threshold is important to symbolise your transition into the world of Nature Magic. Once you cross the threshold, everything you experience and perceive will hold magical messages for you. You enter a different reality, different from your usual everyday reality, a Magic World where trees, animals, stones, landscape, natural features, encounters and occurrences have a symbolical meaning and something special to tell you.

4. Follow your intuition.

   Go where you are drawn to go. Stay where you feel like staying. It's not about walking for miles or climbing a challenging mountain (unless, of course, you feel like it). Staying and simply being in places that attract you can be important. Take time to dream, sleep, enjoy, connect. Trust that you will now, after crossing the threshold, attract special beings and nature energies that will appear in various forms and shapes. They will give you hints about your talents, your purpose and direction in life as well as answers to your questions.

Observe, listen, marvel ...

This is YOUR time! Be open to whatever shows up.

You might stumble across (= finding without searching for it) something special: a stone, a piece of wood, a flower... an object or whatever it might be that is of special importance and meaning to you. If it feels right, ask for permission to take it with you. If you feel a yes, take it with you. Otherwise keep its memory in your heart and mind. It can be a special symbol for your Dreamtime and remind you of your experiences when you are back in your everyday reality.

5. Once you feel it is time to go back, cross the threshold once more, this time in the other direction!

   Take a few deep breaths and welcome yourself back into your everyday reality.

   Disperse the materials you used to build the threshold and put them back to their original place.

Tips:

Before you use this tool:

1. If you are not used to spending a lot of time alone, allow yourself some time to get used to this Power Tool. It can be daunting to spend time alone, in Nature

– yet it is the most natural thing in the world. It is our natural place to be. This is why it is so empowering and balancing. Nature is our ally and teacher and guide. We are Nature.

2. If you feel uncomfortable, it is usually your mind telling you stories. They come from opinions and beliefs that exist in your environment (also see *Unpack your bag*). Try to face your fears and worries. Let them come up.

What is it exactly that you are afraid of? Are you scared that somebody, something will attack you?

Explore the reasons, and let the images that scare you come up. And then look around you, breathe and feel, if there are any indicators that show you signs of danger. Again: Nature is your ally. You are a part of Nature. Nature is your mother, your father, your home. Yes, there are challenges, there are dangers, but when you open your heart and your senses, you will be able to read the warning signs and protect yourself. If you have chosen your place wisely, chances are high that there won't be any unpleasant surprises. In general, nature energies will support you! To experience this is one of the main benefits of this Power Tool.

After you used this tool:

1. Hold back the need to talk about your experience for a wee while. Hold the energy of the messages just within you for a bit, in order to allow them to settle in

and become integrated. Putting them into words can be limiting. Comments from others, even well meant, might be distracting and might dilute your experience, the messages, your images.

2. If you want to, write down some insights or draw a picture, write a song, create something – anything that reminds you of your threshold experience.

3. Sometimes you might not be able to read and interpret the signs and symbols immediately. You do not need to. Crossing the threshold and entering the Magic World of connection with Nature is enough – the meaning will reveal itself in due time.

PRACTISING MAGIC

Code of practise

Uplift and bring balance

Use all Power and Magic Tools to create uplifting things that bring more wellbeing, balance and happiness into your own life and into the life of others. Always ask your Self: *Is this for the benefit of all life forms, not only myself?*

Use your new powers and skills wisely – don't play tricks on others or scare them on purpose. Don't use them to brag or to exert power over others – in the long run this always backfires and will cause trouble in your own life. We are all cells in one big body of Life. If one cell causes harm or stress for another, it affects the whole body – and the trouble-causing cell will suffer as well. Cancer cells are a good example: in the beginning of the dis-ease, it might seem as if they are thriving. But if they can't be kept in check, they spread without control, overpowering neighbouring cells. This can eventually lead to the death of the whole body-system.

Be centered – grounding

Make sure you are in a calm state of mind when you practise your magic skills. By the way: this applies to "normal" power tools as well – never use a hammer when you are upset or an "emotional mess" ;) The likelihood of causing harm to your Self or others increases drastically when you are not centered within your Self.

Stop. Breathe deeply... Listen to the river, the wind in the branches, the birds... Watch the clouds move... Feel the sun or the rain or the wind on your skin... Lie in the grass and feel the earth carrying you...

If you really are in inner turmoil, use one of the breathing methods below or some of the Tools in this book to reach calmer waters (for example *Letting go I* or *Letting Go II*).

Your Spirit Support Team

Call in your Spirit Helpers – regularly.

We all have a support team in the unseen world, no matter if we are aware of it or not. Maybe you have already felt a presence of "some thing" or "some body" that sometimes helps you when you are down or protects you when you are scared at night? Some people call it their Guardian Angel(s), others call it Totems or Spirit Guides – whatever name you want to use: it is a helping energy that comes in many forms (angel, light being, totem animal, pure light etc.). In *Meet your Support Team* you can learn how to consciously make contact with your Spirit Helper(s).

Call in your Spirit Helpers before practising your magic, before using any of the Power Tools, before challenging situations, at the start of the day, when somebody is not kind and nice to you, before a big game or performance or event, when you feel nervous, upset, insecure, unsure – in short: call them whenever you can do with some support! They will be there and connect you with universal Life Energies.

Find a safe and comfortable space

Where you practice can influence your experience. It can make it easier or harder. Practising football on a prepared pitch is definitely a different experience than playing on a stubble field.

Find a place where you

- can focus on your Self
- feel safe
- feel comfortable (you determine what this means in detail, for example warm, relaxed, cozy)
- can express your Self freely and unhindered without having to worry about others.

Temperature and light can play an important role when choosing your place. Make sure you feel cozy and relaxed. Often, darkness or dimmed light can support your practise. There is a reason why shamans, visionaries and healers often used caves or wooden structures covered with animal skins to create a sacred protected space where Magic can happen. Dawn and sunset were and still are chosen times for ceremonies and rituals. Try it!

Natural places can also assist you. River, Lake or Ocean all have a calming and balancing effect on our body-mind-soul-system. They help us to enter worlds of Magic and Intuition and to leave "everyday stuff" aside.

Wear your safety belt

In general, power tools often require safety gear – same here! Make sure you wear your "safety belt", especially when you practise entering different realities. Always tell somebody you trust and love where you are and what you plan to do.

Yes, you have your Spirit Support Team. However, it is important to have a physical human support person or team on the grounds as well – at least for the first couple of years of practise ;)

If you experience any physical or emotional reactions = if you don't feel well: STOP. Don't ignore these important signs, and stop whatever you are doing. Lie down on your back, take a few deep belly breaths and open your eyes to bring you back into your everyday reality. You can also set an alarm or ask your support person to check on you after a certain time.

General practise routines

Before...

1. Relax, become still and center your Self

One of the most effective ways to do this is something we are all very familiar with – we do it all the time: breathing. Our breath connects us with everything, within and without. Often, it is enough to just take a couple of deep long breaths in order to calm down. If you feel upset or deeply unsettled, then you might use one of the following three simple techniques from my book *Dance into Your Inner Light* – they are good Tools to have on board for all sorts of situations and challenges.

Dolphin Breathing 1

Get comfortable so that your breath can flow freely.

Breathe in deeply through your nose and count quietly in your head to four. Hold your breath for four more counts. Breathe out in one strong breath with your mouth slightly open, as if you wanted to blow out forty candles on a birthday cake.

Repeat this breathing pattern in sets of four for as long as it feels good or until you feel calm and settled.

This breathing rhythm is very helpful when you are stressed, tense, anxious, scared, angry or the like. I often use it when I am out and about, have to wait, or when I have to take in and remember a lot of information (it is great for any type of learning and before exams, performances, tournaments, too). I also use it when I need to relax or free myself from bad feelings.

Dolphin Breathing 2

Inspiration: Iruka No Kokyo, by James Deacon

Find a place where you won't be disturbed and get comfortable. When you are ready, observe your breathing.

Feel how it flows in and out of you...

Follow your breath...

You don't have to do anything, just observe...

After a while, imagine a blowhole, just like a dolphin's, on the top of your head. Can you feel it? When you breathe in, it opens wide...

Breathe through the blowhole, in and out...

Feel how the energy flows into your body. It flows through your head into your lungs, into your heart, into your belly... It spreads everywhere and gives your body new energy and strength.

When you breathe out, everything that is not good for you bursts out like a water fountain from your blowhole.

Fresh, strengthening energy flows into your body again each time you breathe in through the blowhole in your head.

Breathe through your blowhole for as long as you can and want to!

This breathing technique not only provides your body with oxygen, but also with cosmic Life Energy. It cleanses you deeply from everything that doesn't serve you. Use it regularly, like a shower, to balance your Self inside out.

If you want to, you can also use the counting pattern from the first technique and see if it feels good.

Power Breathing

Sit or lie comfortably with your back straight.

When you are ready, hold your left nostril shut with your finger and breathe in deeply through your right nostril. Then close the right nostril with your finger and breathe out through your left nostril. Leave your finger on your right nostril and breathe in through your left nostril, and then move your finger and breathe out through your right nostril. Your finger can stay on your left nostril while you breathe in through your right nostril, move your finger again and hold your right nostril closed while you breathe out through your left nostril. Breathe in again through your left nostril, then close the left and breathe out again through the right. Breathe in through the right, move your finger, breathe out left. Breathe in left, move your finger, breathe out right. And again, breathe in right, move your finger, breathe out left, and so on.

Repeat this breathing rhythm about ten times or until you have calmed down.

2. Eyes – open or closed?

Some of us like to close the eyes – it helps with keeping focused and dreaming up things. Others can dream with open eyes ☺ Find out what works best for you.

3. **Set your intention**

As setting a clear intention is so important for ALL things in life, I have dedicated a whole chapter to it (see *Set your intention*).

4. **Call in your Spirit Helpers and connect with Elemental Forces and universal Life Energies.**

As you will see in *Meet your Spirit Support Team*, you have a whole bunch of Energy Beings in your wake that will assist you, *if* you call them in. This last bit is important: they need you to ask them to be able to help you! In order to establish a relationship with them (or one of them), you need to spend some time with them and regularly "check in" – like you would with a good friend. The more you invite them in and make them a part of your everyday life, the more they can support you with whatever you do. Try it out – I am sure you will be amazed.

5. **Ask for advice and guidance from the unseen world while you are practising or doing a ritual to assure that you are aligned with the greater balance and wellbeing of all Life.**

During...

1. Keep breathing deeply (if you remember it ☺)

2. Trust your feelings and simply observe what's "coming up".

3. Follow your intuition (= your tuition from within) and what feels "right" for you in any given moment. If you feel unwell or alarmed, STOP – address those feelings first, before you continue. If needed, seek help from an experienced adult whom you can trust.

4. Don't push your Self – "effortless" is the magic word that describes the underlying feeling of your practise. There are times when we need to push ourselves to overcome challenges, climb a mountain or hold a speech in front of an audience. However, when practising your Tools, when entering "the creative zone", you don't want to do that.

Let things flow freely: Let your constant thoughts and mind images pass by without getting caught up. Let your breath flow freely in and out of your body – just "show up" and be there, holding a space for Magic to enter your conscious reality.

After...

1. Give thanks (Spirit Helpers, Elemental Forces, Father Sky, Mother Earth, ...)

2. If needed: ask for support from the unseen world in your everyday life.

3. If needed: clean up any materials and things you might have used to perform your ritual – ideally give them back to Nature. Make sure that you leave "no disturbing traces".

PRACTISING MAGIC

Tips:

1. Whenever you practise Magic, remember that "Rome wasn't build in a day" and you didn't learn how to walk and talk in a day either. Your magic skills and abilities will grow over time.

2. If you want to be a weight lifter, you need to train your muscles. You start with relatively light weights and gradually move on to heavier ones. To get best results you also probably want to establish a regular routine. The more you train the faster you will see results (= lifting heavier weights, gain muscle strength).

After you have reached a certain strength and fitness, you won't need to train as much and as hard as in the beginning anymore. You will then lift weights that seemed to be heavy at the start with ease. Unless you stop practising with weights completely, you will be able to keep your skills at a certain level. Of course, if you stop lifting weights, your muscles will lose their strength after a while and you will lose your ability to lift much weight.

The Tools in this book are your weights. They will train your magic skills. By exercising your visualisation and intuition muscles, by creating and performing your own rituals and by applying the Tools that you feel drawn to on a regular basis, you will be able to enjoy the many benefits of being a wizard and master creator in Life.

Enjoy the journey. Be gentle with your Self and others. Experiment, have fun and laugh lots.

Power ABC

ABCDEFG

HIJKLMNOP

QRSTUVW

XYZ the alphabet...

Can you remember when you first heard this song? Probably not... You might have heard it hundreds of times since, and reciting the ABC most likely doesn't cause you any headache anymore. You have heard it over and over and over. Then you sung it over and over and over – first bits and pieces, most likely not in the "right" order. You probably had to concentrate hard to know which letter goes where. Until, one day, you could sing it in full length and all. And now you don't even think about it: it is just part of your standard repertoire of songs.

Even if you haven't learned the song, then I assume that you might have learned the ABC (or how to walk) in a similar way: You observed or heard something over and over, then you repeated it over and over – until you could do it. In the beginning you might have struggled, you might have thought, "I will never be able to do that" – but you got there in the end.

Walking, talking, riding a bike, playing an instrument, knitting – whatever it is, I am sure you have many other examples of things you learned in your life so far. Now you do these things with ease and often without thinking.

PRACTISING MAGIC

But there was a time in your life when you fell on your bum many, many times, before you could walk steadily. Remember this when practising with your Power Tools. Be gentle and patient with your Self. Even if you can't see any major progress at first: over time you will gain invaluable skills that can literally change your whole life. Imagine you would have given up when you fell over for the umpteenth time – you wouldn't be able to walk now.

Start practising your magic skills with your Power ABC.

The Tools in this section will give you some ideas of how to call in your power and create Magic in your life. Play around with them, adjust them to your needs, find your own way with them. If you apply these seemingly simple Tools regularly, I guarantee you pleasant surprises.

Rituals & Ceremonies

age 7+

Do you celebrate your birthday?

If yes – why do you do that?

And how do you celebrate it?

Rituals and ceremonies have been used since ancient times to mark special events, experiences, transitions and important moments in life. I am sure you have a special birthday ritual that you love, like having breakfast in bed. Other widely known rituals or ceremonies are baptisms, weddings, funerals and 21st birthday parties.

Humans use ceremonies and rituals to become aware of something special, to celebrate special life events and transitions, to call in support from Spirit World and to transform energies. Ceremonies, rituals and prayers bring healing and balance. They usually work best when you fill them with life, with something that is important to you.

You can create your own ritual or follow some traditional ones – what matters most is that it means something to YOU. Ceremonies, rituals and prayers are your communication devices to get in touch with Spirit World and original Life Energy. They will help you to surf and direct Life Energy in your life in a way that supports you as well as all Life forms.

Rituals often emerge out of the moment or the situation. For example, your birthday is coming up and you plan a special birthday party. Follow your gut feeling and your heart when creating a ritual or ceremony! Here are a few common "ingredients" that you might want to use for your ritual:

Since ancient times, most rituals and ceremonies involve the Four Core Elements – Air, Fire, Water, Earth –, rhythm, song, dance and story telling. Drumming a steady rhythm (also see *Finding my Rhythm*), singing a power song or mantra, using a rattle, listening to the rhythm of Ocean waves, to the steady flow of water in a river or the rain bring our brain into a special state where we open up to Life Energy and Spirit World. They help us to enter a magical space.

If you need some inspiration, keep on reading. You will also find some general guidelines at the end that may help you when creating your own ceremonies.

As said before, the Elemental Forces are strong agents of change and transformation. If you want to mark a special event, change a habit that no longer serves you, get rid of worries, dis-ease, struggles, problems, or if you want to mark a certain point in your life, set your intention in a special way, focus on a wish or dream or project, then working with the Elements can be very powerful.

Four powerful Transformers & Healers

1. Air

You can give your wishes, worries, dreams into the Wind (Air). Wind will carry them away into unseen realms and do its Magic. You can do this in your imagination (visualising), or you can beam whatever it is into a handful of sand, earth, leaves, feathers or any other light natural material, and let it be spread by the Wind. *Imagine how the Wind takes whatever it is that you want to transform and carries it away.*

Air is a great element to take away your worries and fears and anything else you want to get rid of. I often stand in the Wind when I feel "loaded" with stuff or upset or sad, and I ask the Wind to blow away everything that needs to go.

Air also carries your wishes and dreams to "higher realms of Magic". Many cultures used and still use prayer flags to pass their prayers on to the Wind so that they are spread widely and shared with the Universe. You might have seen colourful Tibetan prayer flags around. Often you can buy them in New Age shops. People write prayers and well wishes onto colourful pieces of cloth, line them up on a string and hang them up where the Wind can move them. The Wind will take the prayers (or whatever is written on them) and carry it to the Spirit World for manifestation or transformation.

If you connect easily with the Wind and the element Air, I encourage you to find your own ways of working together with them when creating your ritual.

2. Fire

I don't know about you, but I love Fire. Lighting a candle creates a feeling of solemnity and celebration in me. I also love making a bonfire outside or watch the flames dance in a wood burner.

Fire has a special magic and fascinates humans since ancient times. And Fire is, of course, a great Transformer. The power of Fire can help you to get rid of unwanted things, of anything you want to change in your life. If I want to get rid of something I often write it on a piece of paper or choose an object that represents whatever it is I want to transform or release. Make sure the object is from natural material and burns well. Don't use plastic or other materials that release chemicals or poisonous substances into the Air while burning. I burn the piece of paper or object in the Fire (or in a fire-proof container, for example an empty aluminium can). While I watch it transform I imagine how the energy of it is released and transformed and I am freed of it.

You can also use Fire to release a wish, a dream or a request into the Universe. *Write your wish, dream, request or whatever it is on a piece of paper or choose an object that represents your wish/dream/request (see above) and give it into the Fire. While you watch the flames transforming it, imagine the smoke taking its essence and energy into the Universe... Let it go... and wait for Magic to happen in your life.* A Fire ceremony like this will always set the energetic fabric of the Universe into motion – just wait and see ☺

3. Water

Water is a Super-Transformer as well.

As it is such a big part of our human body (a baby's body is about 75-80% water, and adult body about 65%) and the Earth body (about 71% of the Earth surface is covered with water), Water has a very strong impact. If you can, connect with a *natural* water source as often as possible – not just for ceremony. Water is Life. That's why it is so important to keep our waterways clean and healthy. About 97% of all Earth's water is held in the Oceans. You might not live close to the Ocean, but maybe you have a little stream, lake or even a waterfall nearby. In big cities there often are little rivers or small lakes in public parks or other recreational areas. Of course, you can also use your shower as a ceremonial place. *Imagine where the water is coming from that flows out of the showerhead... Imagine it bubbling out from under a rock in a clear fresh mountain area... It gathers in a little rock pool, padded with soft green moss... It flows down the mountainside, over rocks and into the valley. It forms a river, clear and fresh... Imagine this water now washing over you, cleansing you...*

Honouring Water as a Life-giving force in our everyday life will make a huge difference to our overall wellbeing. Don't just believe me! Try it out!

But let's go back to how you can call in Water to help you in your ceremony. Water naturally is a great "cleanser". Use it especially whenever you have something you want to "wash away". I give you an example: When I was about 11 years old, I lost a very dear horse friend of mine. He had broken an ankle, was in hospital for many weeks hanging in a sling from the ceiling, as he couldn't stand on his legs – and after weeks and weeks of suffering he was put down. I was very very sad. And I was stuck in this sadness for a long time. I had lost other friends and family members before, and the loss of this horse friend of mine brought up all these losses and the sadness at once. I felt really low and dark. Until, one day, a family friend took me to a nearby river. We sat there, looking into the water, watching branches and twigs floating down the river... At one point my friend asked me about my sorrows. I cried and everything welled up in me. After a while, she asked me to throw all my sadness, grief, pain into the river. "Just pour it into the river with all your tears", she said. And I did. In the beginning, I didn't feel much. More and more seemed to come up in me. An endless river of sadness and painful feelings...

However, eventually I calmed down. I watched the water flowing by... I felt emptied out... Empty but very calm and steady. I felt relieved from a huge load that I had carried around for a long time. My friend took her clothes off and asked me to join her in the water. We jumped into the cold water, and she said: "The water will wash away everything that bugs you. Just let it all go." And as we splashed around and screamed (it really was pretty cold), I felt the Water washing away the last bit of grief and pain I had within me. I could laugh and enjoy my Self freely again.

This was my first "water ceremony" that I am consciously aware of. As I love the Water element, I have used the power of Water many times since to help me (or others) find balance and inner peace.

Call in Water whenever you feel stuck with something that doesn't serve you, when you want to change a difficult situation/habit/relationship, when somebody transitioned between the physical and the non-physical world (birth or death) or whenever you want to let go of something.

Take a piece of paper, write your wishes, sorrows, projects, dreams on it, fold the paper into a little boat and let it float down the river. Water will carry it away and restore a "good flow" within you.

Let Water wash over you and imagine how it cleanses all that no longer serves you.

You can also use Water with your prayers: you can "charge" your drinking water with energies you need or want, and you can pass it on to others. In our family we often write words like "love", "joy", "gentleness" or other things we want to attract into our lives on our water bottles. We also put crystals into our jug to load the water with special crystal energies. Check out the work of Masaru Emoto, if you are interested in how this works. He did a lot of research and, amongst other things, photographed the effects of words written on water bottles and music on Water.

You can also make your own Magic Potions and use them for healing, cleansing and balancing purposes (see *Magic Potions*).

4. Earth

Burying something to let it be transformed is very powerful. Buried seeds are transformed into seedlings and adult plants. In many cultures dead bodies are buried to ease the transition from the Physical into the Non-Physical World. People bury the placenta when a baby is born to mark this special event and to connect the baby with the energies of the Earth and the Land. The examples of transformative Earth powers are countless.

The Earth Body can absorb negative energies and change them into growth. You can use this for instance, when you feel angry, sad, down, had a fight or argument or simply want to clear energies in your room, house, school, neighbourhood.

Imagine how you gather all the heavy feelings, all the non-supportive dark energies. Sometimes they are wrapped tight around a person or lie in a thick layer on the ground. Pull them off and compact them into one big pile. Imagine a hole or round channel going down into the Earth. Throw all the dark and heavy energies in it. See how they disappear deep into the Earth. Once you feel "it's done", cover the hole with Earth. The Earth stores these energies. And over time, something beautiful happens, while the energies are held underground: through the Earth magnetic field, microorganisms and other processes they change into life-giving energies!

Use this powerful Element when you want to clear your Self, others, the Land around you from dark non-supportive energies (for example, if you live in a "negative" neighbourhood or in a war country).

Call in one (or more) of the Four Elements to make a powerful stand or initiate change in your life and around you. You will know which one is best for your purpose – trust your gut feeling.

Rattles, drums & more

Rhythms affect our brain activity in a special way. This is why shamans, healers, teachers have used drums to trigger trance states, to travel between different realities, to heal and to enter the realms of Magic. All Life Energy moves rhythmically. Look around you: waves, rain, your steps, your breath, your heart beat all follow a certain rhythm. We can align our rhythm (also see *Finding my Rhythm*) with other rhythms. While playing with different rhythms you will notice how they affect you. Some rhythms will excite you, lift your energies, others will calm you down, harmonise you, or "transport" you into a dreamlike state. Find out how you react to various rhythms before you integrate them into your ceremonies and rituals. They are powerful transformators and need to be handled with care and awareness. I am sure you will find your own way with it. Because rhythm has been used since the beginning of time, it literally runs in our blood. Rattle, drum and chant as much as you like – you will see: it is quite liberating and fun.

If you are interested in learning more about how rhythms and sounds affect our body-mind-soul-systems, you will find interesting facts and research outcomes of neuroscientific studies in the internet (also see *Useful Resources*).

General guidelines and things to consider when creating your own ceremony or ritual

1. Set your intention

In the previous chapter I have already talked about how important it is to set a clear intention in your life (also see *Set your intention*). It is your compass and your message for the Universe what exactly you want.

When you go to a birthday ceremony, you usually express your intention by wishing the birthday child a happy birthday. Before an exam or an important game you might unconsciously set an intention like: "I want to pass this test" or "I want to win this game". Setting an intention consciously and deliberately and creating a special ritual for the occasion makes your ceremony even stronger and more powerful.

Before you start your ceremony set a clear intention about what it is you want to create or attract into your life. *What is it that you wish for? What do you want to achieve?* And most importantly: *Imagine clearly how you want to feel!*

2. Timing

Sometimes, the time of your ritual or ceremony is pre-determined: you will celebrate your birthday, well, usually on the date you have been born into this world. At other times, it might make sense to align your ritual or ceremony with powerful energies that have an influence on Life Energy. One such powerful energy is the Moon.

The Moon has a huge influence on all life forms on Earth as it affects the flow of Water. We humans are "water beings": about 60% of our body mass consists of water (up to 80 % when we are born), our brain and heart are composed of 73% water, our lungs are about 83% water (source: H.H. Mitchell, *Journal of Biological Chemistry* 158). The Moon interacts with our body fluids as it does with the tides in the Ocean. Watch yourself closely over a month: you might notice that you feel "different" depending on the Moon phases. If you follow the Moon phases and plan your activities, rituals and ceremonies around them, your creative and Life-supporting energies will be strengthened and more powerful.

There are four main Moon phases that you can align yourself to: Full Moon, Waning Moon, New Moon and Waxing Moon.

There is a lot to be said about the phases of the Moon. I will only give you a brief overview here. Please "tune in" and feel for yourself how the Moon phases affect you and your environment. Anyhow, it makes definitely sense to align your rituals and ceremonies to the Moon, if you want to increase their effect and power.

New Moon

New Moon is the powerful time of new beginnings. The dark gives birth to the light. The baby is born out of the dark womb of the mother. The day is born out of the night. The energies are building up until they reach their peak during Full Moon. Use this Moon phase to set clear intentions (also see *Set your intention*), to start new projects, to dream up new ideas. Write or draw a picture about what you want to pull into your life. Visualise it. See and feel it as if it is already your reality. Create rituals and ceremonies to anchor the things that you want to attract into your life in your mind and heart.

Waxing Moon

Waxing Moon is the phase between New Moon and Full Moon. This is a time when energies build up. Time to take action, to tackle new things, to make important decisions and to develop your skills. Use the Waxing Moon energies to grow whatever you want to grow in your life, *to* connect with others *and to* realise your dreams. Follow your intentions that you set during the New Moon rituals and allow the energies to move things forward so that your dreams become true. Waxing Moon will help you to be determined, focused and to overcome fears and doubts.

Now is also a good time for harvesting things that grow above the ground, if you want to make *Magic Potions*, tinctures or collect plants to dry for tea or other healing purposes.

The Waxing Moon phase is great for rituals and ceremonies that are designed to support your growth, the development of your dreams and ideas, and to strengthen your confidence.

Full Moon

Full Moon is the time of Magic: the energies are at their highest point and quite intense. The day before Full Moon is a perfect time to send your wishes out to the Universe, to pray for change and transformation, to draw in supportive energies in order to manifest something, to re-charge your Self and your Crystal and Rock friends, and to receive powerful messages and spells to support you in your life.

Be aware of the "dark side" of the Full Moon: you might feel very emotional and/or tense and agitated. If this is the case, use the Full Moon energies to help you create a ritual to release whatever it is that comes up and "bugs" you. Full Moon energies possess transformative power: you might want to sit under the Full Moon and let her light shine on you. If you can't actually do this, because there are clouds, you aren't allowed to stay up or for whatever reason, simply imagine yourself in the moonlight. Let it shine over and through you, filling you up with powerful, strengthening, life-supportive energies and taking everything away that doesn't serve you...

The days and hours before Full Moon are also great to make strong *Magic Potions*, as the Moon's force helps to extract plant energies and their material essence into your potion.

Waning Moon

Waning Moon is the time of releasing unwanted "stuff": quit bad habits, let go of worries, fears, self-doubt, illness, relationships that don't serve you well or whatever else you want to let go of. If you want to detoxify or cleanse your Self or other things, use the Waning Moon energies to ease the process. Shed your "old skin" like a snake – the Moon energies will help you during this phase.

Now is the time to finish off things, to contemplate, to review and to look inside. Create rituals and ceremonies in order to connect with your Spirit Guides to receive guidance and valuable insights, and also to complete things and move on (for example finishing off a project, moving on in relationships, moving house, making changes).

If you are into making your own remedies and Magic Potions, Waning Moon is when you best harvest roots and everything that grows below the ground, as the Moon pushes the energies down into the roots. It is also a good time to preserve and store things for later use.

3. Cleansing/clearing

Before you begin your ceremony, make sure you cleanse yourself (and others that are involved). We always carry "stuff" from our everyday world with us that might weigh us down or distract us. Cleansing helps to leave things that hinder us behind: an argument with a friend, school stuff, etc. It helps us to let go of our load and to be fully present when we enter the invisible realms of Magic and ceremonial space.

Before a regular ritual or ceremony I usually do a "quick cleanse". Before special "one-off" ceremonies that mark a big event or a big transition I might spend a bit more time to prepare myself (also see *Cleansing and clearing energies* for more details). For a quick cleanse you can choose one of the following options:

Imagine white silvery light flowing from the top of your head (some call this point the crown chakra or fontanelle) through your whole body and out through your feet into the Earth. See the light coming from the Universe, the Stars, streaming through your body and washing away all that isn't needed anymore. Breathe deeply and focus on this light shower for a while, until you feel refreshed and clear.

Take a bit of water in your hand and sprinkle it over your body. Imagine that the energy of the water absorbs all that is no longer needed, like a sponge, and clears it away. The Water Energy purifies your whole being.

Ideally, you take the water from a free flowing river, ocean or lake. Doing ceremony outside can add to the power of it and make things easier as you are supported by Nature's energies. However, always remember that the power of your ceremony depends more on your inner intention and focus than on the circumstances around you.

You can also use smoke as a cleanser. Smudging, as it is also called, has a long tradition and is used by many cultures around the globe before ceremony. You need some dried herbs and a fire-proof container. You can make your own smudging stick (see *Make your own Smudging Set*) or buy one. You can also use an incense stick. Either way: be careful as you are operating with the powerful Fire Element. No need to burn down the house or forest when cleansing your Self ☺

Light the incense stick – or dried herbs (I use a Paua shell as container) – and gently blow onto it until smoke starts to curl up. Hold the stick or container in one hand (careful, some containers might get too hot to hold them in your hand!) and use your other hand to spread the smoke over your head and around your body. Imagine the smoke taking away everything that you don't need.

If there are other people involved in your ceremony you can smudge them, too, in the same way. When you are finished, place the incense stick or smouldering herbs in the center of your ceremonial space, on your altar or wherever it feels appropriate. If you want to extinguish them after the ceremony, put the incense stick or herbs into sand or earth – be careful that there are no flammable materials like dry leaves or grass around.

4. Call in your Spirit Support Team

In the next chapter you will find a simple Tool to get in touch with your Spirit Helper(s). If you are already in touch with your Guardian Angel, Totem Animal, Spirit Guide or whatever you call them, then you won't need this Tool ☺

Call in all the energies from unseen realms that you want to be present to support you in your Magic Work. Ask them for protection and guidance: Elemental Forces, the Spirits of the Four Directions (East, South, West, North), the Spirit of the Land, of your family, your friends, your community, your tribe...

You might also want to include special tree or other plant Spirits, rocks, stones or beings that are at or near the place where you want to perform your ceremony. Trust and follow your own intuitive knowing.

5. Create a protected "Magic Zone"

Once you have chosen a quiet and special place for your ritual or ceremony, create a "protected zone" for you to do your magic. I found when I do this, it helps me entering the Magic World and focusing my energies onto things that lie outside my everyday reality.

You can do this in various ways:

- Use a special *Magic Potion* and sprinkle it in a circle (doesn't have to be perfect) around the area where you want to perform the ceremony.

- Use salt instead of the Magic Potion. Salt crystals have cleansing and protective qualities and absorb negative energies (= energies that aren't supporting Life).

- You can also imagine a transparent tube going in a circle around your ritual place. Let a blueish/white light flow through the tube. If you feel you need even more protection, you can imagine transparent walls instead of the tube, filled with the same light. Or even an igloo-like structure that covers your ritual space completely. Again: Trust your knowing and follow what you feel drawn to do.

6. Center your Self

There are many forms to center your Self. You might have your own special method that calms you down and brings you into your center. It doesn't matter what you do: if it works for you – great!

Here a few simple Tools that I use to focus my energies and to ground myself before doing a ritual, ceremony or any other special event that needs my full and undistracted presence:

- *Breathing*

    This is the fastest and one of the most powerful centering Tools I know. I have already shown you a few techniques in *Code of Practise*. You can also simply sit down and breathe deeply into your belly. Close your eyes if this feels ok, and let your breath flow in and out of your body in deep powerful waves. Feel how you draw energy from the Earth with each in-breath into your body... Release any tension, anything that doesn't serve you well, deep into the Earth with your our-breath... Watch how all that is not needed for your wellbeing is swept out of your body on your out-breath-wave... Do this until you feel calm and steady.

- *Earth your Self*

    Sit or lie on the ground in a comfortable position. Ideally you do this outside, on a warm, dry spot, directly on Mother Earth. If this is not possible, never mind: just sit on the floor (if you are bed-ridden, sit or lie on your bed). Place the palms of your hands flat down on the land *(floor, bed)*. Watch and feel how all the energies that you don't need flow from your body through your hands deep down into the Earth... Observe how they are dissolving in the hot core of the Earth... Let the energies flow until you feel that there is nothing left that needs to go... until you feel calm and clear.

Now draw up some energy from the core of the Earth with your hands... Let the Earth energy enter your body through your palms... You might feel a tingling in your hands – that's alright... Swirl the Earth energy around in your body... Bring it into your toes, up your legs, your belly, your chest... into your fingers and arms... your throat... and let it swirl through your head like a whirlwind...

Once you have filled your body with Earth energy, let the energy gently flow back down into the core of the Earth... Feel the steady flow in your palms that connects you to the center of the Earth... pulsating... steady... always...

If you have used this Earthing Tool a couple of times, it will only take you a few moments to "earth" or ground yourself.

7. Perform the ceremony

Your ritual or ceremony is a gift to your Self and all Life. There are templates = rituals others have done before you, and you can draw inspiration from them. However, you don't have to! You can create your very own rituals that have meaning to YOU. There are ancient rituals and ceremonies that got their power by people performing them with great belief and enthusiasm for a long period of time. If you have the chance of being a part of such a ritual, you will feel the age-old power and energy that is called in through the ritual. The power of a ritual depends on what people see in it. The ritual is like a frame for a picture that is painted by you, by people in contact with the Magic World. In a way, the ritual is also a portal into Magic World.

Some pointers for you when creating a ritual or ceremony:

Find something that helps you to focus on your intention (*why do you want to perform this ritual?*) and allows you to be 100% present. This can involve making a *Medicine Wheel,* calling in the Elemental Forces and creating a Fire, Water, Earth or Air ritual (see above) in order to transform certain energies within or around you, or anything else that you feel drawn to. Let things float away, burn them, spread them with the Wind, burry them, write your wishes on prayer flags or simply break a stick to mark the breaking of an old habit that doesn't serve you well. No matter what you do: The power of ceremony is, that it has meaning to YOU, that it is something that is alive for YOU.

Trust your knowing. Always remember: Deep inside, you know all this already. You don't need instructions and manuals. You *know*! Follow your heart and what feels "right".

8. Give thanks

Sounds simple and obvious, but we often seem to forget it: saying thank you and feeling grateful. Gratitude is a powerful feeling and another transformator in our lives (also see *Power Codes*).

No matter if you feel it straight away or not: the Universe is reacting to your ceremony, your Spirit Helpers will spring into action, Life Energy will align to what you "put out there". Expressing your gratitude, feeling thankful for your connection to the unseen world will open the pathways and channels so that more "goodness" can flow towards you.

Set your intention

age 7+

Setting a clear intention is one of the most important Tools to achieve what you want. I use it every day, in the morning, before I start my day. I also set an intention before making decisions, when planning things, at the beginning of the year, before important meetings, when I start a project… and always before doing any "Magic Work".

Setting your intention has an effect on your brain: as you will see in the chapter *Building new pathways*, your focus and attention influence the wiring of your brain. So if you set your mind, your intention on something, it will create a neuronal pathway over time that allows you to bring into your life whatever you want.

Your imagination will allow you to step away from your current default settings and move towards your dreams. Setting your intention also calls in all your Spirit Helpers and Guides from the unseen world.

In principle, this is an easy-to-use Tool that doesn't require a lot of practice. Make it a regular habit, like brushing your teeth in the morning, and it will help you to keep your balance and focus.

Imagine you are the owner of a huge ship. Before the ship leaves the harbour, you need to get clear about the purpose and the direction of the journey. Otherwise it will just be tossed about in the waves.

Why do you want to leave your "home shores"? What do you want to achieve, see, experience? What is the dream, vision, goal that you are following? Do you want to find new land in the ocean, like Christopher Columbus? Do you want to reach a certain island or town or an already known continent? Are you on the journey to do "business", to learn something or to realise a special dream/ plan/ project?

What are you setting out to do? And why is it important to you?

The answers can be small and humble: "I want to play with my brother today, because I have been quite rude, and it hasn't been nice for both of us."

Or big and bold: "I am going to be a professional football player, because I feel happy and joyful and so at ease, whenever I play football. It feels like 'this is where I belong'."

You can set your intention for the next hour, for a day, month, year, or your whole life. Like the ship owner you might have one intention for a particular day and others for a longer period of time. Intentions can also change. The more aligned they are, the more direct your journey. If you set an intention to go right today, for example, and follow that direction, and then intent to go left tomorrow, your ship will zigzagging on its course. However, it will, eventually, reach the shores somewhere.

Setting your intention will give you a clear direction and help you to realise your dreams faster and more direct. It will keep your ship on course.

I set an overall intention for my life: All I do and am shall raise awareness of how all Life is interconnected. This is my "anchoring point", my beacon that I follow and that gives me direction. When I have important decisions to make, I can come back to this intention and make sure that all I do – the project/plan/adventure – is aligned to it. By focusing on this intention I also call in experiences that support this intention.

I set an "intention for the day" each morning as well. This is a more short-term intention to call in the support of my Spirit Helpers and to consciously call in certain energies into my life: "My intent for today is to be gentle and patient with my Self and others." Or: "My intent for today is to find a good outcome for everybody involved in the team."

Setting an intention will not only keep you on track, it will also make it possible to realise your dreams, to be true to your Self, and to call in Magic and the help and support from other realms. Setting an intention has an impact on the non-physical and the physical world. Let's go back to the ship. You, as the owner, set an intention where to go and let the captain of the ship know. The captain and his crew will then follow and carry through your intention, say sailing to Africa to deliver some seeds, for example.

Every time you set an intention, your mind (captain) and body (crew) will have a clear path to follow. Your intention will act like a magnet that will attract the energies around you into this "field of intention".

It can be fun and helpful to create a ritual for yourself each time you set an intention to underline the importance, to be fully present and to help your mind to take it in and remember it.

This can be as simple as lighting a candle while you say out loud what your intention is. You can also create your own "intention ritual", as small or as grand as you like. For long-term intents you might want to create something "tangible or visible" to re-mind you over time. This can be a picture or a collage of pictures, a drawing, some lines in a journal, an object, something that represents your intention – anything, really, that reconnects you with your original intent.

Tips:

1. Ask your Self: *what do I crave more of? How do I want to feel?* Distill it into one word. One word that evokes a feeling and gives you a sense of what it is you want to achieve/get/be.

2. Become aware of your "Monkey Mind". If you are like me, your mind floods you with thoughts and ideas all the time. Like wild monkeys in the jungle they cajole through your consciousness. It never stops. And if you don't know how to manage your mind, it might go wild and wreak quite a bit of havoc. Setting an intention gives you a focal point that you can come back to when your mind goes wild. You can reign your Monkey Mind in and give it something to play with: your intention. You can also use the simple Tool in the chapter *Monkey Mind* to help you focus.

3. As said before, setting an intention will call in all our Spirit Helpers. It will also often call in obstacles! It is like the Universe is saying: "Great, you want this? Here is what you still need to clean up in order to make space for it." So be prepared this might happen! Roll up your sleeves and get to work: these obstacles are a chance to reclaim your power! Overcoming them will create the necessary space for your dream. Challenges can be a chance to move your attention off what's happening around you: instead of "I want the world to be different", "they shouldn't be doing this" or "why is this happening to me – this is unfair" consciously

bring your attention within, into your body, your heart, your belly and nourish the stillness inside of you. There is nothing to fix! Your interactions (and potential obstacles) will change automatically if you connect with this place of stillness inside of you. Use the *Diamond Power Station* to strengthen your connection to your inner power center.

4. And last, but not least: Set an intention every time before you practise or use any of the Power Tools in this book!

Meet your Support Team in Spirit World

<mark>age 5+</mark>

You are not alone!

Your mum and dad might have gone into town, your siblings (if you have any) might be at a friend's house, in school or wherever, your pet might be sleeping on the couch and not seem to notice... in short: you might *feel* alone, but you never really are.

Ever heard about Spirit Guides? Some call them Guardian Angels, Totem Animals, Light Beings or Spirit Helpers. You can call them whatever you want. Important is that you get in touch with them. They are your support crew in Spirit World. As you might know, not everything in this Universe is in material form. When we are born, we enter the Material World and live in a physical body for a certain period of time. We come from "Spirit World", and this is where we will go back to when our physical bodies die. In Spirit World we find the essence of all Life in various energy forms, that is: without a physical form. Spirit World is pure energy. That means: you cannot touch it, grasp it, but you can *feel* it.

When we grow up, we get more and more caught up with "physical stuff". After all, this is what we came for when we were born: to experiment and learn in physical form. We learn how to use our bodies, how to think, play and plan with our brains and how to create "things". So it is easy to lose sight of Spirit World, especially if you grow up in a setting where the contact to Spirit World is not part of everyday life.

In many indigenous cultures around the globe Spirit World is a very real and honoured part of life. People make time to connect with Spirit World, to listen and to get guidance, for example when making important decisions or looking for orientation.

Spirit World is always there and is always a part of Life. If we want, we can consciously connect and stay in touch. Why would you want that? Because there are many Spirit Beings or energies that can and want to support you. I will give you some examples: Have you ever just sat there, looked out of the window, and, all of a sudden, an idea popped into your mind? Or have you felt the presence of a loved one around you who did no longer live in a body? You might also have felt the presence of a pet who died? This is, because the energy of our loved ones is always with us, no matter if they are still around in their bodily form or in Spirit World.

There also are Spirit Guides, Totem Animals or Guardian Angels. They are Energy Beings from Spirit World who choose to be our support crew. They help us in our physical form. We are all connected to at least one, often more. These Energy Beings come in all forms and shapes. They can change over time, so you might not always see the same Spirit Guide when you use the following Power Tool.

How can you get in touch with them (if you aren't already, of course)?

Well, it is a bit like in our physical world: if you want to get in touch with a friend or loved family member, you need to call them, right? The same applies with Spirit Beings, even more so: they usually wait until we get in touch with them! They don't "call" us on their own. They might send gentle and subtle signals and messages, but if we don't react and make a connection, they will leave us – seemingly – "alone".

This Power Tool shows you a simple way of getting in touch and making a connection with your Spirit Guide(s). Like good friends and family members your Spirit Guides are always there for you, but you need to remember and make time to connect with them, call them into your life, so that they can support you. Once you have made contact and established a relationship, you will see how easy it is to simply chat with them and ask them for advice.

Spirit Guides see things from a wider perspective than we do. They are not limited to human restrictions. They include all living things, not only humans, which means they can share precious insights, and their advice goes way beyond our own view and the view of the people around us.

Are you ready? Then come and meet your Spirit Guide(s)!

Indigenous people all over the world use drums and rattles or anything else they can find (voices, sticks, stones) to create a steady rhythm. Rhythm affects our brain activity and energy flow and carries us to a place where we can dream easily. It helps us to open up to whatever wants to come into our conscious mind.

You can use this Tool without drumming, however, you might know someone experienced in *shamanic journeying*[1] who can drum for you and/or guide you through the steps. You can also use a recording (see some recommendations in the chapter *Useful Resources*) to ease the way and help you to enter your Dreamspace.

Whatever way you choose: rest assured that your Spirit Guide is already waiting for you and looking forward to meeting you!

1. If someone is drumming for you, he or she will know when to start drumming. If you use a recording, then start it now.

2. Find a feel-good position and close your eyes... Relax... Listen to the drumming... or to your breath (if you do it without drumming).

    You don't have to do anything... Just relax and breathe...

    Ask your guide(s) to show up...

    Then just wait and breathe, listen and observe what happens...

3. Stay as long as you want.

   If you want, you can ask your guide for answers to questions you might have or for advice. You can also ask your guide(s) to show you anything that is important for you to know right now.

4. When you feel the meeting is over, give thanks to your guide and slowly make your way back into your everyday reality.

   You will know when the meeting is over and when it is time to open your eyes.

Tips:

1. When you use this Power Tool for the first time, it can be really helpful to have someone who has experience in shamanic journeying or in guiding meditations to assist you. It will make it easier for you to concentrate on meeting your guide. The more familiar and used to it you get and the stronger and clearer your relationship to your guide becomes, the less you might need additional resources for your meetings.

2. Your guide may choose to appear in various forms and shapes. Don't worry about it, and simply take it as it comes.

3. The lengths of your meetings will vary: The more used you get to meet your guide(s), the easier you will find accessing Spirit World. Go as often as you like and need to, and stay as long as you want.

4. One precautionary advice: In Spirit World, as in our physical world, there are not only well-meaning Spirits and energies floating around. Be aware and follow your inner gut feeling: If something doesn't feel "right", if something doesn't feel "good", STOP! It's important to know, that you can always set boundaries and stop the meeting! If something feels strange, come back and open your eyes. This is true for any meeting, no matter if in the physical or in Spirit World.

Having said this: by setting a clear intention to meet your Spirit Guide before using this Power Tool for the first time, you instantly create a protection wall that only invites supportive spirits in – so you should be fine. Later, when you already know your Spirit Guide(s) well, you will be able to detect any "disruptive energies" and Spirits that might not be supportive. And: your Spirit Guide(s) will keep those energies away as well.

Building new pathways – Cycles

age 8+

Strictly speaking this isn't a Tool – it rather is a "user prescription" that helps you to get the most out of everything you do in life. As you might have noticed, life comes and goes in cycles. One example is the seasons of the year: spring, summer, autumn, winter. Another one is life, childhood, teenage years, adulthood, old age. As all things alive we are bound to these cycles, and it makes our life a lot easier and smoother if we follow them. Planting strawberries in mid-winter isn't such a good idea. However, if you plant your seedlings according to the seasons and – even better – aligned to the Moon cycles, they will grow and flourish and share their fruit abundantly.

Your body naturally follows a lot of cycles, too. Observe yourself and you might be surprised. Some people are affected strongly by the seasons: there are summer-people, who love the heat and are most creative and active when the temperatures are high. In winter their systems "shut down" and their activity levels literally freeze. Others are paralysed by the heat and much prefer the winter cold. Winter is the time when they get active and creative and are at their peak.

As we are "water beings" (our body consists of 60-70% water), the Moon also has a strong influence on us. You probably know how the Moon affects the ocean tides.

She also influences our body fluids. Observe yourself and others close to you, how the Moon affects you all. It may show in many forms, sometimes only very subtle and hardly noticeable, sometimes more obvious and visible from the outside.

I noticed that the Moon cycles have a strong impact on me. Before and around the Full Moon I usually need time to retreat, to be on my own, to reflect and to look especially well after myself. During and after the New Moon I am much more active and outgoing. This is a good time for me to make important decisions, have meetings, start or continue to work on projects and meet with friends.

In general, the Moon phases affect our mood, our activity levels, our whole wellbeing. Knowing your "Moon rhythms" will allow you to adjust your movements and to keep yourself balanced and well. Observe your Self over the period of one Moon cycle, and I am sure you will be able to notice your Moon rhythms.

Another influential cycle process in our life is the wiring of our brain. It happens throughout our whole life whenever we learn or experience something new. While we grow up, we create neuronal pathways in our brain that influence how we live our life. Usually this happens without us being aware of it. I will show you how to consciously manage and influence the neuronal pathways in your brain, so that you are in the driver's seat of your life, following and creating the roads that you want to drive on, rather than going down roads that lead you to places where you don't want to be.

Imagine a natural forest or jungle. If you look closely, you will find some animal tracks. They lead to drinking holes and feeding places, to places for resting, sleeping and playing. Otherwise the forest is untouched and in its natural balance. No roads, pathways, sign-posted tracks.

This is a very rough metaphor for our brain and its neuronal pathways when we are young. It's mainly untouched terrain. During the first few years of our life we are busy creating new pathways in our brain jungle. Whenever we learn something new, we activate or create a neuronal pathway in our brain that allows us to do whatever it is we want to do in an easy and smooth way. When we learn to walk, for example, we practice the first step over and over again – until we "got it" and our muscles react directly and instantly to the signals they get from our brain. Like creating a pathway through the jungle by walking a certain path over and over again, until the small overgrown track is transformed into a decent path on which we can walk easily and fast.

Our mind has a strong impact when we create new pathways in our brain. It is like a machete that cuts through the thicket. This is why it is so important to manage the mind and our thoughts consciously to avoid damage and hurt.

If your parents, teachers or somebody else in your surroundings tell you again and again that you are good at something, they install a belief in you: "I can do this". With your "CAN DO"-machete you will, over time, establish a pathway and wire your brain accordingly. As a consequence, you will become better and better. Naturally, this also works the opposite way! If your surroundings aren't supportive, it will create beliefs of "CAN'T DO", "I am no good" or whatever else it is. And if we are not aware of these detrimental beliefs and thoughts, they will cut through our brain jungle wildly and randomly, sabotaging and destroying and leading us astray.

This is why it is so important to become aware of the activity of our mind: of our thoughts that form into beliefs and create neuronal pathways that affect our reality (also see chapter *The Monkey Mind*). Learn how to manage your mind and guide it consciously so that it becomes a useful rather than a destructive tool that messes things up and randomly creates pathways that don't serve you.

Some points to consider:

1. Building a pathway takes time. Nobody learns to walk in a day. Allow at least 21 days for the creation of a new pathway: Do whatever it is you want to establish *continuously* for at least 3 weeks. Some pathways may take longer, depending on the terrain and circumstances. Just keep walking on them.

   The more you walk on a new pathway, the "wider" (= easier to use) and more stable it will become.

2. Use this process

   - Whenever you want to do something new or in a new way.

   - When you want to change existing pathways, for example when you have a habit that doesn't serve you well. A habit is an already existing pathway through your brain jungle. Some habits are useful (for example the habit to brush your teeth), but some aren't beneficial for us (for example a running technique we got used to that doesn't allow us to run as fast as we could).

- Whenever you notice something that you want to change because it doesn't serve you (or others) well, and simply reverse the "cycles" process: instead of walking on the "old habit" path, you now actively focus on creating a new pathway that will, eventually, make the old one obsolete. To do that, you need to a) STOP yourself whenever you realise that you are walking down the "old" path, and b) FOCUS on the new pathway that you want to create instead. Imagine what you'd rather be doing, how you'd rather act or react in a certain situation, etc. Repeat those two steps – stopping yourself and focusing on walking a new path – over and over, and you will create a new pathway in your brain and energy field. And, like in the jungle, the less you use the old pathway, the more it will overgrow until you won't use it at all and it won't be visible anymore.

Power Codes & Magic Spells

age 7+

Do you know that you already have a very powerful and sharp Power Tool in your toolbox? You don't have to acquire it, you don't have to "set it up" – it is already there and chances are that you use it all the time, without paying too much attention to it. In this chapter I will show you how to use it consciously, as a Magic Wand and Power Tool.

The Tool I am referring to is: language or words. Words are Power Codes; they are Magic Spells. You can use them to create different pathways and conjure up whatever you want in your life.

Let's do a little experiment: Read the following words (you can read them aloud if you want) and observe your Self. *What do you "see" in your mind? How do these words make you feel?*

Ready? Here we go:

"dumb"

"idiot"

"stop it"

Observe the pictures that each word paints into your mind. Allow some time for this.

When you are ready, read the following words:

"thank you"

"let's"

"joy"

Again: Observe how you feel when saying each word.

Did you notice any difference between the first and the second series of words?

Words paint images into our heads, and their sound transmits messages into our body. This affects how we feel. If you learn how to you use words and language wisely, you will become a Word Wizard, creating magic as you go. This is why wizards, shamans, healers all over the world use spells, mantras, prayers, invocations. Words are powerful. We are one of the few species on this planet that uses sound in this form (dolphins and whales are other examples of Sound Wizards using sound patterns in a very elaborate way).

In this chapter I will show you a few basic Power Codes and Spells to start your magic journey. I will also show you how to protect your Self from words that others might throw at you – consciously or (in most cases!) unconsciously. Most people aren't aware of how they use their words. They copy the language and words that they heard in their surrounding when growing up, without thinking about it. This is natural. If there is a lot of swearing and coarse language around you, you kind of have to develop a "thick skin" in order to "survive" in such an environment. Over time you will get used to the swearing and accept it as your "normal".

Observe your Self: What happens when you are teased? What happens within your Self when people swear (at you or around you)? How does it make you feel, deep inside?

Or don't you feel anything? Do you "close down" and shrug it off?

Compare this to the feeling when somebody says something nice about you, praises you, acknowledges you, gives you kind advice, comforts you...

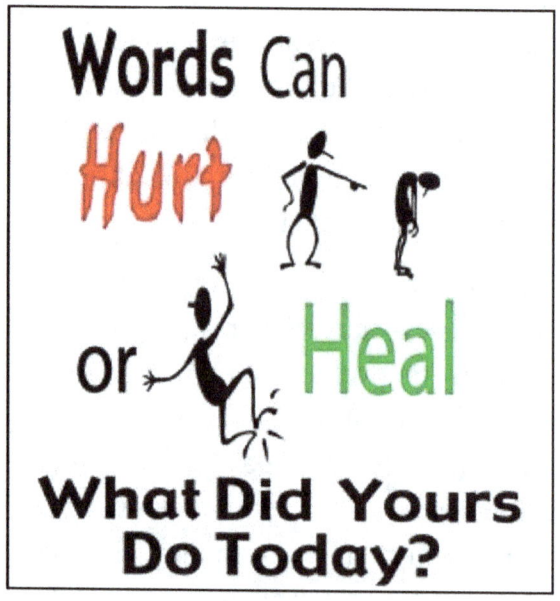

Power Codes

The following might not seem like magic Power Codes at first glance, but I have seen their power again and again. Simple tools are often the most efficient and commonly used tools. Big complicated machinery is something for specialists: you mostly have to practice long and hard to be able to use it, you need safety gear, and it takes some preparation and effort to set it up. Let's start with "simple and powerful".

1. Words of gratitude

"Thank you for being my friend." – "Well done! Thank you for helping me with this." –"Thank you for taking me for a hike in the mountains. I am so happy I did this."

I have a little ritual that I do every night: Before I go to bed, I look back at the day. I watch the events and experiences pass by like in a movie, and at the end of it I try and pick as many things as possible that I feel grateful for. It doesn't have to be big stuff. In fact, when I had a "not so good" day, it seems that the dark clouds cover my whole sky and I can hardly find anything that fills me with gratitude! The spotlight of my thoughts seems to focus on the unpleasant things. So I gently and deliberately turn the spotlight into another direction and ask my Self: what am I grateful for today?

Sometimes I have to poke little holes in the blanket of dark thought clouds to let some bright rays of gratitude shine through. Over the years I found that there are *always* bright rays, even when they are hidden behind the dark sky: I am always grateful for having a safe shelter where I can sleep at night. I am grateful that I have food and clean drinking water. I feel grateful when I think of the Sun that warms my skin, the Rain that brings water and cleanses the land. I feel grateful that I can hear, see, feel things... And all of a sudden, more and more rays break through the darkened sky. There are rays everywhere, until my whole sky is bright and illuminated and I am filled with gratitude. I *love* this process. It literally makes my day every time I do it! No matter how dark and exhausting my day, no matter how frustrated, sad, depressed, angry I felt – this little ritual always leaves me feeling good.

In the beginning it might take some convincing your Self to actually do it. But once you established a routine and experienced the changes that happen if you do it regularly, I am sure that you won't want to miss it anymore! It really creates Magic and is one of the easiest-to-use and most efficient Tools I know. The mechanism is simple: you focus on things you are grateful for and fill your Self with gratitude. As you have seen in *The Monkey Mind*, the images and thoughts that we carry in our head and heart influence how we feel. And how we feel creates our reality. You act like a magnet: If your energy field is filled with dark thoughts and images, and if you feel low and not well, this is exactly what you will attract more of. If your energy field is filled with bright and light images and feelings, your magnetic field will attract more and more positive stuff into your life!

Try it!

What are you grateful for right now?

2. Words of kindness

We probably all know the warm fuzzy feeling when somebody says something nice: "Well done, you did a great job!" or "I am so glad you are my friend." Words that express love, acknowledgement, respect, compassion naturally are strengthening and nourishing. And usually we – or others – need to hear them most, when we feel down or dark and not in balance.

Next time when someone is snappy or glares at you, smile and say something nice. This also works when *you* feel grumpy and surly! Say something nice to your Self! Instead of answering back or kicking your brother, acknowledge your Self. We *all* have our moments, we are *all* triggered at times – and there are always "masters" around us who push our buttons. They make us aware of the areas that aren't in balance – thank you very much ☺

Be nice to your Self. If nobody else around you seems to understand and to support you, take yourself away and be kind to your Self! Breathe, feel the "good things" around you, focus on your *intention*, be gentle, patient and compassionate and say something kind to your Self, such as "Come on, have a rest." Become your own best friend!

3. Magic Spells

You might have read about wizards and enchantresses using Magic Spells. Magic Spells are normally used to transform or transmute something, like turning a prince into a frog or so. You can transform pretty much everything you like. Words are Power Codes that paint images into our heads, and as I have explained before: the images and thoughts we carry determine how we feel, and how we feel determines our reality. Words can also affect us through sound: the sound enters our energy field and changes its frequency. So use your words and sounds wisely, and they will be powerful Tools to help you to consciously shape your reality.

A common "mistake" a lot of us make is: we want to transform external things. Let's say you have ongoing trouble with a friend. Instead of fighting you'd rather have fun and enjoy your friendship again. Trying to transform him or her into wonder-man or wonder-woman most likely won't get you there. It is much more efficient if you start with your Self. Why? Because everything is created from the inside out. This is how energy creation works: from the non-material into the material. From thought and mind-images into dense matter and physical form. As within so without.

Something within your Self has created or allowed the troubles with your friend. You might even have created this unpleasant situation, unconsciously, to learn something specific from it. So changing your friend won't help! He or she is just a reflection of something inside of you that needs to be seen and learned. Start with looking inside and transforming your Self.

When I was about 18 years old, one of my teachers told me to start the day by standing in front of the mirror and saying these Magic Words:

"I love my Self."

"Say it a couple of times and repeat it as often as you can during the day", she said. To be honest: at the beginning I found this a bit awkward and strange, and I couldn't *feel* the words at all. So I stopped doing it – until much later in my life when another mentor reminded me to use this powerful Spell again. "Fake it until you make it", he said, when I told him that I didn't really believe in these words and couldn't feel the truth in them. As I didn't feel very happy at the time and as it was relatively easy to do and didn't take much time I gave it a try nevertheless. Whenever I felt stressed, insecure, challenged, sad, angry, out of balance, I repeated the words "I love my Self, I love my Self, I love my Self" in my head or aloud. Over time it became a new habit. I did it whenever I thought of it, many times a day, but especially when I didn't feel well or when the going got tough. Little did I know that I was using one of the most powerful life-changing Magic Spells.

I soon noticed the changes within and around me. I felt better, happier, calmer, more confident. And, as a consequence, I attracted more and more supportive and feel-good things into my life.

Try it! I am sure you will create wonders in your life by using this powerful Magic Spell.

Another great and effective spell is:

"I am."

This Spell helps you to gather or reclaim your power. Combine it with a couple of deep conscious belly breaths and visualise your Self in an ocean of energy, connected to all that is.

"I am!"

You can use this spell in many different situations. I find it helpful when I get nervous before speaking in front of a large audience or when facing a challenging situation. I also use it when there is conflict "in the air", for example before (or during) a challenging meeting or a conversation I dread.

Tips:

1. Use your words wisely! They are Power Codes that shape your life. Swearing and disrespectful words send out a specific energy, as do kind and respectful words. What kind of energy do you want to cultivate in your life?

2. Train your Self to use Power Codes (words, spells) that make you feel good, empower you and paint positive images in your head: "I feel peaceful" (instead

of "I am not nervous"), "I want to be healthy and strong" (instead of "I don't want to be sick and unwell"). It will make a HUGE difference. Try it!

3. Don't point your finger at others. Start with clearing your own energy field – and focus on keeping it clear.

4. Combine Power Codes (single words, spells) with visualisation and breathing. For example: Imagine a mountain, its strong and calm presence, when you use the "I am"-spell (or anything else that makes you feel calm and strong inside). Breathe deeply while you say the words and focus on the picture in your mind. Breathing opens us up and helps us to anchor desired energies in our body.

Cleansing & clearing energies

age 5+

Have you ever felt a "bad atmosphere" when coming into a room where two (or more) people just had a fight? Or when you had an argument with you best friend, or your siblings or your mother...

Have you ever felt "heavy"? Or sad? Or "all fired up"? Or exhausted?

While surfing the waves of Life it sometimes happens that negative energies well up and leave their traces – within ourselves and around us. When we dig in the dirt, we get dirty and need to take a shower – or at least, wash our hands. When we walk in the city, we get dirty from car exhausts and all sorts of human-created "pollutants" in the air. When we had a fight or experienced something that left us with negative energies, or when we are in a place where people left negative energies, we need an energy-cleanse in order to stay healthy and well.

Objects and places absorb energies as well, and it might be a good idea to "clear the air" whenever you feel it's needed. The following simple Tools will help you to clear energies within yourself and also around you.

1. Clearing energies with water

Sprinkle water over yourself and visualise how all the sadness, anger, frustration, worries, aggression, exhaustion, "not so good feelings"... whatever it is that you want to clear is washed away by the water drops trickling down your body. See how the water absorbs the energies like a sponge and takes them down into the Earth. The Earth will neutralise and dissolve the energies.

If you have access to a river or waterfall, live close to the ocean or a lake, you can also go for a dip, and splash water over you. Feel how all the energies that don't serve you are washed away and dissolve deep down in the Earth. If it is in the middle of winter and too cold for you to swim (however, there are ice swimmers in Russia – so no excuses), just scoop water up in your hands and splash it over your head. If you don't have a natural water source close-by or cannot go there, use your tap water at home.

If you want or need to do a deep cleanse, take a bath with Epsom salt (you can get it in some supermarkets or health stores). Imagine how the energies dissolve in the water and are absorbed by the salt crystals (make sure to give the bath tub a good rinse after your cleanse). You can also jump into the shower and visualise how all the unwanted energies leave your body and are washed away, down into the Earth where they dissolve...

2. Clearing energies with light

Visualise a bright light (the colour will come to you – I usually see white or golden light) pouring down from the Universe. It enters your body through the top of your head and flushes through you. It swirls around within your body and fills it with pure clear light.

Do this until you feel completely cleansed and entirely filled with pure light.

3. Clearing energies through the Earth

Ideally you do this outside where you can directly touch the Earth. If you can't do this for some reason, then do it wherever you are and imagine your hand is connecting to the Earth below you.

Sit on the ground and place your palms on the Earth. Imagine how all the unwanted energies flow through your hands down into the center of the Earth and dissipate there... Let the energies flow until you feel it is done...

If you want, you can then recharge yourself with Earth energy. It will give you inner strength and bring balance after an exhausting or not pleasant experience. Leave your palms flat on the ground (as before) and draw some of the Earth's core energy up through your hands and into your whole body. Watch how the energy is sucked up, and then spreads throughout your cells. See how it is swirling around through your entire body, from the soles of your feet up to your head, and back down to your feet.

Now let the Earth energy flow out again through your palms... taking everything that doesn't serve you with it, deep down into the center of the Planet...

Feel your connection to the Earth... Take some deep belly breaths and feel clear strong Earth core energy pulsating through your hands into your body, and back out again... This connection is always there for you when you need it...

4. Clearing energies with smoke (smudging)

Smoke is an ancient method to cleanse people and objects from unbalanced energies. As said before, Fire is a very powerful transformator. Shamans and healers use it to get rid of "bad energies" in healing ceremonies. People used to burn things that were said to hold negative energies. Witches were burned because people believed that only the power of Fire is able to transform or dissolve the negative energy of witchcraft. Fire and smoke (also see *Make your own Smudging Set*) are still widely used in healing ceremonies and to cleanse negative energies. If you go to church, you might have seen how smoke is used to clear sacred space for prayer, traditionally with frankincense.

To clear energies with Fire or through smudging you have a few options:

- You can burn objects that carry or symbolise energies that you want to clear. The fire transforms the unwanted energies and they will literally end in smoke.

- You can write all the things that you want to "go" on a piece of paper and burn it.

- You can also clear energies with smoke. Fan smoke all over your body to cleanse yourself after a fight or to prepare yourself before you do something important. You can also clear the energies of a place with smoke. Imagine how everything that doesn't serve you/the place/others well is carried away in the smoke and dissolves into thin air.

You don't have to burn down the house and make a big fire in the lounge in order to clear your space or yourself! You can, however, make a bonfire outside, if you want to – and if your parents/guardians are ok with it.

I love bonfires. They are very powerful and can teach us a lot. If you don't want to or can't make an open fire for whatever reason, incense or smudging sticks are a great option. You can get incense sticks from crystal shops, health stores, Asian stores, some supermarkets. If you want, you can also make your own smudging stick.

Before you light your incense stick, make sure that hot ashes and burnt materials won't fall on a flammable surface (for example: carpet, wooden floorboards, sofa, table...). If you can, go outside. If this is not possible, or if you want to clear a room or house, take care that you hold a plate or something inflammable underneath the stick.

Once you are ready, light the incense stick.

Gently blow on it to nurture the flame with your breath. Your breath connects you to the Fire energy. Let the flame burn for a few seconds, then gently blow it out. The incense stick should now spread nice-smelling smoke.

Point your stick to the East, the South, the West and the North to honour the Spirits and the energies of the Four Directions. Now point it upwards to the Sky-Father, and downwards to the Earth-Mother. Call their energies in and ask them to help you with the clearing.

Let the smoke swirl around you by moving the incense stick carefully around your whole body. Imagine how the smoke takes away all the unbalanced energies and transforms them...

When you feel "it is done", thank the Spirits of the Four Directions, Father Sky and Mother Earth.

If you want or need to, you can ask them to fill your body with their strengthening energies and their love. Watch the smoke as it weaves around you and imagine how it fills you with nurturing energies...

Once you are done, extinguish the incense stick by putting it into the earth or a bowl of sand. You can also leave it burning: put it in a bowl of sand, an incense holder or simply an old glass, vase, cup, and let the smoke cleanse the place. (Please consider: the rim of the container might get burnt/blackened by the heat of the burning stick = take one that nobody uses anymore.)

Tips:

1. If you want to clear the energies of a place – a room, a house, your neighbourhood, a whole village/ street/ city/country... –, you can use the Tools described here and simply apply them to the place instead of your body. Visualise how the power of Water/ Light/ Earth /Fire cleanses and transforms the energies of the place or the whole area.

2. Objects absorb energy. If you wear your favourite T-Shirt all day, it will be impregnated with your energy at the end of the day. The same is true for jewelry, furniture and pretty much everything else that you use: you will leave your energy traces wherever you go – like a smell your energy will attach to objects and other living beings. And the energy of other people will attach to you. If you are not cleansing it, it will stay. All is good if the energy is "nice" and supportive, like a pleasant smell. If not – well, you might want to get rid of it.

I often buy secondhand clothes. It happened a couple of times that I felt "strange" and even unwell when wearing my new attire. I learned that energies aren't always cleaned away through normal washing! Sometimes, energies are literally stuck in the fabric, especially heavy ones such as grief, sadness, anger, and washing alone won't do the trick. I use the Tools above to give new clothes a good cleanse.

The Tools are also helpful

- when you got things handed down from your siblings or friends
- when you move into a new place
- when you had a fight or an unpleasant situation
- when you had a "bad day" (or others around you had one)
- when you feel unwell, sad, restless or frustrated
- when you need healing
- before you perform a ritual or ceremony

3. As usual: trust you feelings and intuition! If something feels right, follow that path. If something doesn't: don't do it!

Protection

Why do people wear helmets when riding a mountain bike down a steep hill? Or shin pads when playing football? Or gloves when pruning blackberries?

Every now and then we find ourselves in situations where it is wise to have some protection to maintain the wellbeing of our body. A lot of people protect their bodies with clothing, shoes or other protective gear, and, in some cases, with weapons. But what about our mind and soul? There are three pillars that support our being:

It is important to know how to protect not only the body, but also our mind and soul. If somebody says something mean, for example, it can often do as much or more harm in the long run than a physical attack. Sometimes Spirit energies are "stuck" in a place for a long time, and this can affect us in a not-so-good way if we aren't aware of it. War, deep conflict, fights, sudden deaths, violence, aggression or depression leave their invisible energy traces behind. You might have heard people talk about a "haunted" place or house.

If you are a sensitive person, you probably feel those energy traces, for example when you pick up a "bad atmosphere" entering a room where people have had an argument. You might feel uncomfortable and not at ease when coming to a place where something dramatic has happened in the past. No matter if you are aware of it or not: the energies have an effect on you, and it is good to have some Tools on board to protect your Self.

In this chapter I will show you a few Tools you can use to do this. They are also helpful to prepare and protect your Self and your space when you do rituals or ceremonies, and, in general, whenever you feel the need for your own safe private space.

Tool 1 – Magic Cloak

Imagine a blueish-silvery cloak with a hood. It completely wraps around your body and covers it... The cloak is made of a special shiny fabric that reflects all energy that comes towards you back to where it came from... The blueish-silvery light is a protective layer that surrounds your whole being.

Nothing can come through to you and affect you, unless you open the zip of the cloak... You are fully protected and safe in your own energy field...

Tool 2 – Golden Egg

Imagine an egg-shaped membrane of golden light surrounding you... The light bubble is wafting around you like a soap bubble... Even though it is soft, it is unbreakable.

The golden light is pulsating through the membrane creating a strong protective field around you... No harmful actions, words or even thoughts can penetrate through this gooey rubbery golden light bubble... You are completely safe and strong in your own power field...

You can also use this Tool to protect your loved ones – people, animals, objects – no matter where they are. I protect my bike from getting stolen in this way, when I leave it in town. You can also use it to stop bullying, when people treat you in an unfair or harmful way, and in general whenever you feel that you need protection from negative energies that are directed towards you: anger, frustration, annoyance, stress.

Tool 3 – Energy Shield

This Tool is similar to Tool 2. It is simple and very powerful. I use it mainly for "other things" = not to protect my own body-mind-soul (I prefer to use the Golden Egg for that). I find it very effective to protect my Self and others from collisions, for example when driving: cars are fast machines, and we humans are far from having things "under control" when we drive around in them. If you live in a rural area like me, all the "road kill" tell a story about this.

I also use this Tool before I board a plane, train, bus or ferry. It is great in places where many people come together (schools, events, festivals, performances, sports activities) to protect your Self from energies that might affect you in a negative way. If you are like me and get distracted quite easily, it will help you immensely to stay centered and true to your Self and to keep your boundaries.

Imagine a bright white light-shield around the person/object you want to protect... It looks like glistening white mist floating around the person/object, similar to the corona of the Sun.

You can make this corona as large as you feel it needs to be.

When I drive I usually extend it quite a bit in every direction in order to protect the car from being hit or hitting others (for example birds, rabbits, deer).

Tips:

1. Be aware of the energy flow – everything is energy. Even though our energies are all connected, we each have our own energy.

Your energy field is made up of millions of individual energy fields.

You and your siblings and your mum and dad form the energy field of your close family.

Many families and your neighbours form the energy field of your community.

Many communities form the energy field of a country. And so on.

And: There are billions of other energy fields, apart from our human energy fields, that affect our personal energy field which on its own is made up of the energy fields of our cells which are made up of the energy fields of molecules and atoms and so on... It is like a gigantic jigsaw puzzle made up of gazillions of individual energy fields. Imagine that! Pretty mind-boggling, isn't it?!

2. You can roam the infinite space of Life Energy and commingle with Life Energy in its various forms by using some of the Tools in this book. However, you also came into this physical existence in order to experience how your individual energy field interacts with other energy fields around you and how to create new energy fields. In order to do this safely, you sometimes need to protect and define your own personal energy field(s). The Tools above can help you to do this.

Use them as safety and protection Tools in your everyday life, when you experiment with the Power Tools in this book and when you practise your Magic skills.

Power Tools for every day

In the previous section *Practising Magic* I shared some Tools and exercises for you to set up some basic routines that will help you to create a magic life. In this section you will find some easy-to-handle practical Tools that you can use in everyday situations to ease your journey through life. If you get used to them, you can build a solid platform with them from where to face challenges, retreat to and maintain your balance.

As with everything: practise and perseverance will make you a master.

I recommend that you pick one or two Tools at first and focus on them for a couple of weeks. Give your Self a good chance to become familiar with them before you move on to other Tools.

Letting go I

I don't know about you, but I sometimes have things in my life that I'd rather not have. It might be a dream that haunts me, it might be some memories of a not-so-nice situation or experience, it might be worries or fears that bug me and keep me awake at night... Or somebody really pushes my buttons... We always have a choice how we react, of course. But I find it not always that easy to reign in my emotions and ground my Self ☺ It takes a bit of practice, but with some of the Tools you are given here you will be able to do it.

A Mongolian shaman showed me this Power Tool, and I used it ever since to neutralise thoughts or mind pictures that pop up, so that they no longer trouble me. It is also very effective to deal with "unfounded" worries and fears that come up again and again. Sometimes, it can be useful to dig deep and find the underlying reasons behind our fears and worries. You can do this, for example, with the support of your *Spirit Guide* or with your *River teacher*. However, at times we carry worry and fear deep within our cells, and they need to be released or neutralised when they arise. This simple Tool will help you to do just that.

1. Whenever the pestering thoughts, worries, fears pop up, find a safe and quiet space. Sit, lie or stand in a comfortable position and keep your eyes open.

2. Breathe deeply and slowly, and move your head from left to right like this:

   Breathe in – turn head to the left side

   Breathe out – turn head to the right side

   Turn head back to the left side and then to the right side *without breathing*

   Breathe in again – turn head to the left side again

   Breathe out – turn head to the right side

   Turn head left/right without breathing

   And so on...

   Find your own rhythm that feels right to you, and keep doing it until you feel calm and settled.

Tips:

1. Visualise your fears, worries, memories, troubling dreams in detail while you do the breathing and head turning. Continue until they fade away.
2. Should the fears, worries, memories, troubling dreams arise another time, just use this Tool again. Over time they will go away for good!

If they don't, there is mostly an underlying message somewhere hidden in them. Try to find the hidden message – you can do this together with your Spirit Guide(s), or ask a person you trust for some support. Once you know the hidden message, your fears, worries, etc. will usually stop.

Letting go II – Riding wild horses

age 8+

Here is another great Power Tool to help you deal with emotions that overwhelm you. It is all good and important to "let off steam", to cry and shed some tears, to yell out loud when you are frustrated – as long as you do not direct your "energy in motion" (e-motion) towards other people or your Self and affect them or your Self in a non-supportive way. It can be helpful to go into the forest, the garden, your room or to retreat to a safe place where you can be alone and cry, literally scream your heart out and let everything come up (and out) that boils and brews within you. Often after an "outburst" like this you will feel relieved and liberated, calm and more settled.

This Tool can support you whenever you feel that certain energies come up again and again and affect your Self and others in your life in a not-so-good way. The energies might be so strong that you feel overwhelmed by them. They gallop through you like wild horses in a stampede – and can potentially harm your Self and others.

Let's learn how to ride and calm the wild horses within ourselves.

1. When you feel things are "boiling" inside of you, when you feel like being swept away in the midst of a strong current of energies and the "horses" gallop wildly through you, make a conscious effort and STOP. If need be, take yourself away from the situation or

from somebody and retreat to a safe calm place. Bathrooms are good ☺

Close your eyes.

If you feel that you need some support with this ask a person you trust to remind you and to encourage you to "step away", to close your eyes and to guide you through the steps below. Set your intention to use this Tool regularly – it will make it easier.

2. Feel into your body. Where do you feel the energies?
3. How do they feel?

Soft, hard, painful, taking your breath away, aches or tension in the heart, neck, back, stomach, knee...?

If you don't feel anything, stay with this feeling of "emptiness", "blankness"...

4. Do your energy-horses have a particular colour?
5. Observe your body...

Let the horses run free and watch them... Feel where they are in your body...

6. Keep your eyes closed and watch the horses until you feel them settling down...

Energies in motion and horses both have something in common: after a wild race they *always* settle down and go back to grazing in the end ☺ Trust this process – and remember it when you feel the horses going wild.

Tips:

1. In case you find this Tool a bit tricky to use at the start, don't worry: you are not the only one! Learning to ride wild horses is a great adventure – and certainly not an easy task. It might take a while until you manage to take yourself away and to close your eyes. However, I encourage you to keep trying. It is really worth the effort. This Tool can help you to deal with strong energies that could otherwise have a negative effect on your Self or others.

2. As always in Life: use your common sense = don't close your eyes when you are standing at the edge of a cliff, raging inside ☺

3. This Tool is also very useful when you are nervous before an exam, a tournament, a stage performance, a speech or presentation in front of a crowd. Athletes often use it to release "emotional pressure", for example before a free kick in football or a serve in tennis.

   The more you use this Tool the more adept you will become and the faster you will be able to "calm your horses".

4. The most powerful "motor" to set energies in motion is fear. Fear can trigger an outburst of rage and aggression; it can make you feel really sad or depressed or panicky. Sometimes, you will be able to dive deep into your Self and find the fear behind your

emotions. You can do this, for example, with the help of your Spirit Guide, with your Rock friend or by sitting with River or Tree.

Getting to know your fears is very empowering and important. If you know your fears, you can address them and deal with them consciously. This will affect your relationships: the relationship to your Self, to others, to other life forms, to Life Energy itself. Like many other challenges in Life, fear disappears when you face it and deal with it directly.

5. It also happens that things in our surroundings aren't in balance: family, friends, people we meet who haven't faced their own fears and aren't aware of their energies in motion. People who are overwhelmed by their own hidden fears. This might affect you in a negative way! It might be that your fears are caused by these circumstances. If you feel this is the case, please connect with a person you trust. If you are unsure or if you don't have a person you trust, ask your Spirit Guide(s) for help. Your Guide(s) will send you support. Open up and look around for people who can assist you. There often are groups (at school, church, local authorities), Help Lines and organisations around that offer advice and active support.

Your Magic Power Place

age 5+

Whenever you run around with lots of ??? In your head, when you feel restless, not sure about things – in brief: whenever you could do with some loving advice and guidance, this is a simple yet efficient Tool to use.

1. Take a few deep belly breaths.

2. Imagine a wonderful place where you can relax and are completely at ease... A place where you feel safe and comfortable... A place where you love to be...

   This can be a place that you already know. Or it can be a place you dream up.

   A warm sun-filled beach with turquoise waters, a mountain meadow, a forest clearing, a cave, your comfy bed at home... Choose one special place that makes you feel good.

   Imagine it with all your senses: what sounds do you hear? What smells do you smell? What do you feel in your body? How does the ground feel under your feet?

3. Sit or lie down in this place and enjoy the feeling of comfort and peacefulness...

4. When you are ready, call in your Spirit Helpers and invite any other supportive energies.

5. Then simply sit (or lie down) and wait... enjoying the place...

6. Breathe deeply... Your helping Energy Being(s) will show up sooner or later. You can also imagine them, if this is easier for you.

   It might be a familiar being (for example your Spirit Guide or Totem Animal) or it might be a new energy form that you haven't met yet.

7. Welcome whoever turns up; then ask if they are willing and able to help you. If they agree, share your question or story with them.

8. Wait and see what happens... They might show you something; they might take you on a journey; they might answer you in words, images or ideas that pop up or cross your mind; not always immediately... Allow time!

   Be still, breathe deeply and listen inside... Let Magic happen...

9. You will feel when the "meeting" has come to an end. Thank whoever is present for their support.

10. If you want, stay a bit longer in your magic Power Place and enjoy the stillness there.

11. When you are ready to leave, come back to your awake-reality. Stretch your body and make sure you take things easy for the next hour or so. Ideally, you spend time outdoors or have some quiet time for yourself.

Tips:

1. Remember: Your Power Place is always there for you. You can go there whenever you like, no matter how wild, unsettling, frustrating, depressing, chaotic, crazy, sad things are for you. It is your very own retreat space where you can find peace, guidance and loving assistance. Always.

2. Make sure that nobody will disturb you while you are visiting your Power Place. I used to lock myself into the bathroom or climb a tree to be "out of sight" from other family members for a while…

3. If you have a Power Place in your physical everyday world that is easily accessible – great! I have a place near our house where I can hear the river whispering, feel the mountains in my back and look out over the ocean. I actually go and sit there often, because it strengthens my connection with helping energy forms. The natural environment literally rebalances my whole body-mind-soul-system.

However, as said before: your room, the bathroom, the attic, a tree – all work just fine as a platform to visit your magic Power Place inside of you. Enjoy!

Talking with the Rock Family

> age 7+

Have you ever collected interesting rocks?

I love walking at a rocky beach exploring all the differently shaped and coloured pebbles. And I love finding crystals in the mountains. Rocks and minerals are amongst the oldest Beings on this planet. They have been here for eons of time: most of the Earth's rocks formed millions of years ago. They are the building blocks of Mother Earth, and the platform we stand on in more than one way. Because they have been here for so long, they hold a lot of wisdom and have many valuable qualities.

Humans used rocks for tools and weapons since ancient times. Nowadays, quartz crystals are widely used in technology, for example in computers to store information. They have the unique ability to convert electrical energy into mechanical energy and vice versa. This is called "piezoelectric effect" and is used in modern technologies: sonar, radios, cigarette lighters, transistors, computer chips, LED displays, digital watches, satellites, microphones and many other electronic and digital devices are based on "Crystal Power".

Rocks, crystals (gemstones) and minerals are also able to influence energy fields. This is why healers and seers use them as a healing and divination tool. In the Native American tradition, medicine women and men used and still use them to communicate with Spirit World.

Have you ever been drawn to sit on a certain rock, or to pick one up? Rocks call us! And if we are open, we will *feel* their call. Rocks can tell us a lot about a place. I have learned interesting facts about the places I lived in or traveled through just by listening to the stories of the rocks there.

As you can imagine, rocks have a very different frequency from ours: they are much slower, much denser than we are. In order to talk with them, we need to learn their language. I often sit or lie on rocks, and – after some time – their stories "pop up" in my head. It is very interesting to listen to them – try it! You might learn some fascinating facts from times long gone about the places you live in or visit.

The following Power Tool is a great starter tool to get in touch with the Rock Family (if you aren't already). It's simple and fun to use, and it will teach you to understand the language of the Rocks.

1. Come up with a question.

While you are still learning Rock language, it is often easier to receive an answer on a specific question.

2. Let a rock find you.

Don't search for it: instead, be where you are (this can be in your garden, in a park, in a forest, at a river or beach, on a mountain). Wander around or sit still. Be present and open, and trust that the Rock who wants to connect with you will show itself.

In most cases it will – sooner or later. Your attention will be drawn to it, you will suddenly spot it, tumble over it ... No matter how: you will feel "this is the one" ☺

3. If it feels right, pick the rock up and hold it for a while.

   How does it feel in your hand?

   Close your eyes – it might help you to "tune in" more easily.

   Does it have a smooth surface, a rough surface? Does it feel warm or cold, wet or dry, heavy or light?

   What shape can you feel? Round, edgy? How does it smell? What do you hear when you hold it close to your ear? Something – nothing?

4. Now open your eyes and look at it.

   What colour does it have? How does it look like: has it many sharp edges, soft corners, ridges, stripes, patterns...?

   Explore the rock and record as many details as you can.

   <u>Note:</u> If you want, you can do this step with a friend, family member, school-mate or with a whole group of people who are open to play with rocks. You can also do it on your own, of course.

   If you do it with a partner, share your observations with him/her. Describe what you feel and see: surface structure, shape, special features (for example small cracks). Mention how it feels when you touch it and anything else that pops up for you, and let your partner write down what you said.

If you do it without a partner, write down your own observations, talk about them aloud while recording it on your phone or another device (in case you don't want to write or not be distracted by writing). Important is that you will somehow remember all the details later on.

5. Once you feel there is nothing more to explore, take a few deep breaths and hold the rock quietly. Simply sit with it for a while.

6. Whenever you feel ready, go through your notes or recording and revisit each observation one by one.

What is the rock telling you?

Think of your question (step 1).

Explore your question and the rock's answers: Find out how your observations relate to your question.

This process can be quite interesting together with a partner, as he/she might "see" things and connections that might be hidden to you. If you do it with a partner, state your observations (for example: "I see a white circle on the upper part of the rock" – "The rock feels smooth, it has just one rough corner", etc.), and let your partner write them down. Once you have finished your observations, go through the notes together and see if the meaning in relation to your question shows itself.

7. Once you feel "complete for now", thank your rock friend and ask it if it wants to be returned to its original place. If you get a yes (you will feel the answer inside of you: the more you practise, the clearer you will "get" the answer), take it back. If you feel it wants to stay, you can keep it and it might be your companion for a while. Remember to say thank you and always treat it with care and respect.

Tips:

1. Rock beings are wise old beings who hold a lot of energy, knowledge and wisdom. If you want to practise your Rock language skills, lie down on a big rock or boulder, close your eyes and breathe deeply.

   Feel how you slow down... and slow down some more...

   Relax... Don't do anything. Let your thoughts pass, if there are any...

   Allow yourself to deeply sink into "Rock Speed"...

2. You will be surprised what you will learn! If you open up to them, Rocks might not only answer your questions, they might tell you stories about the ancient history of a place. I found out a lot of interesting facts about the area we live in by listening to rocks. We live near a "crystal mountain" with a lot of quartz. The rocks - small and big - gave me a

picture of how the land looked like thousands of years ago, long before humans touched it, and also shared stories about the humans who walked the land centuries ago.

3. Rock language is very slow and very different from any human language, so we have to get used to it. From my experience, it uses a lot of pictures rather than word-like structures. Sometimes the meaning of a Rock message reveals itself only days or weeks or even years after you received it! That is Rock Time for us humans ;)

4. Be patient! Learning any language takes time! It probably took you ages before you could utter the first few words in your mother tongue. If you have a baby sister or brother or little children around you, you know what I am talking about. Being immersed in a human-made sound bubble within our first years of life we slowly pick up a few distinctive syllables or words that seem to stand out in the world around us: *ma-ma, pa-pa...* And over 2 to 4 years we acquire a more or less sufficient pool of words to a) have a rough idea of what others are trying to tell us and b) to get our messages across. On average, it takes us 2 to 4 years to come to grips with our human language! And during all this time, we usually hear that language constantly around us. Please remember this, when you want to learn Rock or Tree or Bird or any other language!

Crystal Magic

In the previous chapter *Talking with the Rock Family* you have heard about the unique ability of quartz crystals to transform electrical energy into mechanical energy and vice versa (piezoelectric effect). This is why they are widely used in modern technology. But Crystals (gemstones) and Rocks also have many other qualities that they might share with us if we treat them with respect and care. Crystals store energies, "memories of times long gone" and consciousness or spirit matters, and they can influence energy fields! This is why they have been used for healing, divination and all sorts of magic and sacred ceremonies and rituals since ancient times and why they have also played an important role in alchemy[2].

Many native peoples, shamans and healers revere Crystals as special beings who express the unity of the five elements: Earth, Fire, Air, Water and Spirit. Spirit is the fifth element, the "glue" that binds everything together. Crystals grow deep in the womb of the **Earth** and form much of the Earth's crust. Crystals are fiery, too: some are birthed through the power of **Fire** (volcanic activity), and some are directly linked to the Sun or other Star energies. Their piezoelectric properties are another sign of their relation to Fire. Crystals are transparent and allow light to flow through them or they reflect light

(**Air**). Yet Crystals are also closely linked to the element of Water: their hexagonal molecular structure resembles snowflakes, and some of them look like ice crystals.

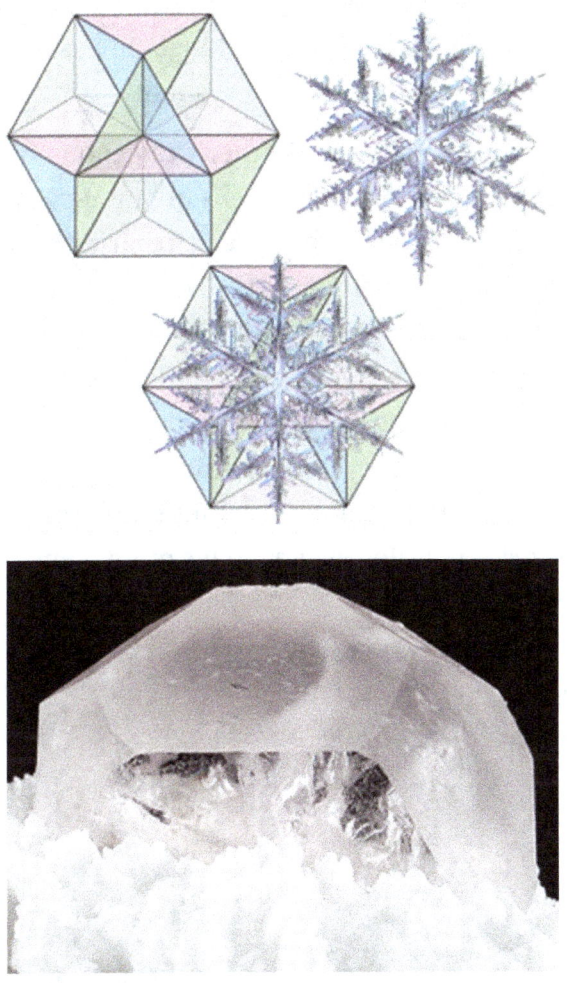

Indigenous peoples see the Earth as a living being: Rocks such as Granite and Sandstone are forming the skeleton of the Earth's body. The Earth's crust and the soil are like the skin of her body. Mountains and Rocks wear down over millions of years to become soil, rich in mineral nutrients. Plant root systems and waterways are the veins of the Earth's body through which the "lifeblood" (Life Energy) flows. The Mineral kingdom is taking on the role of the nervous and sensory system.

In Native American and other indigenous traditions, Crystals are seen as the brain cells of Mother Earth. They form her "Brain Mind" through which Spirit, the Universal or Cosmic Mind, communicates with all parts of the Earth's body and regulates all Life-important functions such as temperature, hydration, etc. Because of these and other unique properties of Crystals, anyone who can tune into the energy of Crystals is said to be in tune with Mother Earth and also able to communicate directly with "Spirit World" in order to expand his or her consciousness beyond human limits.

Crystals will speak to you in your own way, as they are able to tune into *your* energy. There is not one way to communicate with them. Make time to sit with them. Simply feel them in your hand – and over time, you will develop your "own way" and mutual language to exchange information. They can be great teachers, advisors, guides, friends, companions, protectors.

1. Cleansing Crystals

As said before, Rocks and Crystals are very powerful. This is, amongst other things, because they are so good at absorbing (storing) and emitting energy. Be aware that they also absorb "negative" energies. I have met quite a few rocks who absorbed "war energies", as they had been taken from battlefields where people had fought and suffered. They also often take in the energy of natural disasters or human-created energies like vibes of conflict, depression, and aggression. Be mindful of that, especially when you get them from crystal shops and don't know where they come from.

Crystals can also become "fully charged" and saturated with energies. Sometimes this can even change their physical appearance: your Crystal might look "cloudy" and not very clear.

In order to de-charge negative energies and to restore their full capacity, you need to regularly cleanse your Stone and Crystal friends. As described in *Cleansing and clearing energies*, it is essential for our wellbeing to get rid of energies that don't serve us from time to time. The same is true for our Crystal companions. It is best to do this before you start working with a Crystal or Stone, and *every time* you do a special ritual or feel the need to do it. It's a bit like having a shower: every now and then we need to have one to cleanse our body ☺

The simplest method to cleanse your Crystal or Rock friend is under running water. Water is balancing for every living being and it realigns troubled energies. You might have experienced this yourself when taking a relaxing shower or bath after a stressful day or when you go for a swim in a river, lake or in the Ocean.

If you have a natural water source nearby, place your Rock in the current and let the water wash over it. You can also use tap water, if you don't have access to a natural water source (don't use it if it is too chlorinated though). While the water runs over the Rock, imagine how everything that "clogs the system" of the Crystal now floats away with the water until the Crystal feels bright and clean again. Sometimes I leave Crystals or Rocks in the river near my house for a couple of days or even weeks. Trust your "gut feeling" that will tell you when the cleansing is complete.

There are other methods of cleansing a Crystal or Rock: you can smudge them (see *Make your own Smudging Set*), bury them in the Earth, let moonlight or sunlight[3] shine on them or place them in a bowl of hematite stones. You can also visualise how everything that doesn't enhance the core energies and balance of the Crystal flows down into the Earth and dissolves.

Once you are more fluent in Crystal and Rock language, your Crystals and Rocks will tell you what is best for them at any given moment, but in general, cleansing them under running water is a very effective, easily accessible and simple way.

2. Recharging and programming Crystals

If you want to recharge your Crystal, you can place it in Full Moon or New Moon light – best outdoors or on the windowsill. You can do this for a night or for several nights. Talk to your Crystal friend and trust your intuition: you will know for how long.

The Moon has a huge influence on all life forms on Earth (also see *Rituals & ceremonies*). Your Rock friend will appreciate the powerful and balancing energies of the Moon.

When you place your Rock on the windowsill, be careful that it isn't exposed to sunlight for long hours! Most Crystals and Rocks I have met don't like to be in plain sun light for too long. Especially not when lying behind a glass window.

You can also program your Crystal with your intention. This can be useful whenever you want your Crystal friend to support you with something, for example to protect you from negative energies around you. I have a few rose quartz Crystals that help me to protect my energy field when I work at the computer. They absorb the energy radiated out by the computer, so that I am not affected or harmed by the radiation. Some people attach little Crystal pendants to their mobile phones to reduce the radiation. I also use obsidian and other Crystals when I am speaking in large groups or am in meetings where people have conflicting opinions to protect myself from "getting sucked into" negative energy fields, and, most importantly, to be able to keep my own energy field up and intact. Crystals can be valuable helpers to balance conflict in your family or in school.

When you use Crystals for protection or balancing, make sure that you give them a good cleansing after they have been exposed to "disturbing energies". As they absorb these energies, it is important for them to release them again and to have a rest. I forgot to do this with one of my oldest Rose Quartz friends: she got all cloudy and "fogged up". I buried her in our garden for a couple of months, and then cleansed her in the river – and she completely transformed and was all clear again.

To program your Crystal hold it in front of your third eye (the place between your eyebrows on your forehead) and ask it to do whatever you want it to do. For example: "Please protect me from negative energies around me, and keep my energy field clear." Focus and concentrate on your "request", visualise what you'd like to see, so that your Rock Friend can pick it up and follow through. When you feel it "got it", say thank you and place it where you need it to be (near the computer on your desk, around your neck, in your pocket, in your room...).

Like a good friend, treat your Crystal with respect and care. Check in with it regularly, especially when it is doing some work for you ☺

3. Healing with Crystals

Rocks and Crystals have been used for healing purposes since ancient times. Going into details and explaining the various healing properties of Crystals would go beyond the scope of this book. If you are interested in this, you can contact me or do some research yourself: there are many good books written about Crystal healing. In this chapter I will give you just a few pointers to start your explorations.

Crystals are not only able to heal our bodies, they are also great to balance the energies in our houses, gardens, neighbourhoods ...

Crystals have helped me

- to heal bones (I taped them onto my broken ankle),
- to keep the energy field in my house balanced (I place them all around the house, in my office, in the lounge, in the bedroom – they are great dream guides, too),
- to restore the balance in my garden (I place or bury Crystals and Rocks in my gardens to keep soil and plants healthy and happy),

- to channel and direct energy (that's why some healers and shamans use Crystal Wands) and

- to clear land from negative energies that are stored there from past times (there are a lot of places around the world where conflict has happened, for example in form of land wars or other battles; natural disasters can also leave disturbing energies in the land).

Follow the guidance of the Rocks and Crystals and trust your intuition. They will tell you what to do and where to place them! The more you work with Crystals and Rocks, the better you will understand their messages and learn their language that is so different from ours. If you are a "Rock person", they will show you ways to assist your Self and others in this life. Be patient and allow time! It might not happen over night – or it might, if you are closely linked to the Mineral Kingdom!

Dream with your Rocks. Ask them to send you messages while you sleep. Talk with them as you would with a good friend. Take good care of them. Treat them with respect. Play with them and get to know them well.

4. Communicating with Crystals

First: you will find your own way of communicating that works for you. Make time to sit and play with your Crystal or Rock and get to know them. Do what feels right – and gently push doubts or nagging voices away ("you are just imagining this", "this doesn't work", "rocks aren't alive", "they can't talk"). Those kinds of thoughts come from your mind and are usually influenced by your environment. If they pop up, just ignore them. If your mind needs some "food for thought", try this: French geologists Arnold Rheshar and Pierre Escollet believe that Rocks have a sort of "vital activity". The two scientists say that although Rocks are different from plant and animal life, they also change and grow old.

When I want to communicate with a Rock or Crystal, I normally do the following:

a) If it is a big rock or boulder, I sit or lie on it and allow myself to "do nothing". I slow down my breathing and become very still. Smaller Rocks or Crystals I either hold in my hand, or I place them on my forehead (between the eyebrows). Sometimes, I feel the urge to place them on my belly or other body parts. Again: trust and follow your gut feeling. There is no "right" and "wrong".

b) I breathe deeply and slowly into my belly, until I feel relaxed and calm. I signal my wish to get to know the Rock and to communicate with it. Then I simply wait and see, listen, feel...

You can also ask a question and, in general, talk with the Rock as you would with a good friend. Your words or thoughts will automatically translate into Rock language. You just have to learn how to understand and interpret the messages the Rock is sending back to you. Allow time for this! Eventually, you will become more and more fluent in Rock language and easily pick up the messages. As Rocks are sending on a slower frequency than humans, it might take a long while (in human-time) until you get your reply. And it might come in various forms: imagery, dreams, thoughts that seem to pop up "out of nowhere"... You will get used to it and be able to understand the messages more and more clearly!

Tips:

1. Where do you find Crystal or Rock friends?

    Well, look around you: they are literally everywhere! You do not necessarily have to go to a Crystal shop and buy expensive crystals. They can be found on forest tracks or on pathways in a park (gravel on pathways often comes from quarries, and sometimes you can find really nice quartz pieces). You can meet rocks near a river, in your garden, on mountains, at the beach... Once you open yourself up to the Rock Kingdom, you will be surprised where you will find them – or rather: where they will find *you*!

    - Set your intention: "I want to meet a Rock."
    - Then let it go, clear your mind and just follow the law of attraction: go where you feel drawn to, and follow your gut feeling. Trust that the Rock/Crystal will come into your life at exactly the right time.
    - Once you have found your Crystal, ask if it wants to come with you. Sometimes, especially when you

find Crystals outdoors, they want or need to stay where they are. You can still talk with them, visit them, play with them. But only take them with you if they signal that they are ok with it – you will feel a "yes" or a "no" deep inside of you. Trust your feelings!

2. As is true for all relationships, your relationship with your Rock and Crystal friends might change over time. Sometimes I "lose" a rock, or I feel the need to pass it on to somebody else or to bury it in the Earth. Be open to change and ready to move on and to let the rock go. Letting go of something "old" creates space for something new to come into your life.

Breathing with the River

age 5+

River is a great teacher.

Whenever I need to make an important decision, whenever I need clarity or answers in tricky matters, whenever I need a break because things are simply "too much", I always go to River. I sit on a stone, dangle my feet in the water (yes, even in wintertime; it's freezing, but very invigorating – try it! Not for too long, though), and I listen to River's stories. We are lucky to have one right next to our house. But even in big cities there often are little streams or rivers in parks and recreational reserves.

I won't make too many words in this chapter: River will do all the talking and magic work with you – just give it a go.

This Power Tool is very easy to use, and I am sure you will find your own ways of using it, together with River.

1. Find a river.
2. Sit with the river. You can also lie on a big stone in or alongside the river. If it is warm enough for you, you can, of course, also sit or lie directly *in* the river.
3. Listen to the river.

You might talk to the river and explain why you came, but usually the river and the whole environment will pick up where you are at and how you are feeling pretty easily, so you do not have to say anything unless you want to. Important is, that you then stop and listen. Listen to the river.

Sounds easy – it is!

Don't do anything, if you can help it. You can play with River later. For now, just listen and allow River to weave its magic.

Breathe deeply and follow your breathing, if it helps you to relax.

Tips:

1. The more often you do this, the easier you will probably find it to "wind down" and to just listen and tune into the river. You will learn the language of the River. Like with learning any language, it might take a while, or you might pick it up very easily and fast. Just enjoy the process. The better you become at understanding River language, the easier you will get answers, guidance, insights. River will give you peace of mind and heart.

2. River is usually a gentle teacher. However, especially after a heavy rainfall, she can be highly energetic and wild, too. Respect her. When she is wild, be careful around her. Like with humans, too: when they are "wild", you better listen from a safe distance ;)

3. Of course you can extend this Tool and use variations of it: Sit and breathe with Ocean, Lake, Tree or Mountain. Once you find this easy and got used to their languages, sit and listen to birds or any other animals in your surroundings.

Diamond Power Station

age 7+

This is a very powerful Tool. I learned it from a dear friend of mine, Chong-Mi Müller. She is a great healer and wise woman and taught a lot of people how to use it to strengthen their inner power center. "If your inner center is stable and strong", she said, "you can be more gentle, compassionate, calmer and powerful in your relationships and in your whole life."

This Power Tool will enable you to consciously shape your experiences. You can use it for literally every area of Life: friendships, family, health, sports, school issues, projects, jobs, ...

1. Find a comfortable and quiet space.
2. Sit upright – on the floor or on a chair, important is a straight back – and breathe deeply into the center of your belly.
3. Place one palm on your belly button, the other palm on your back, directly opposite of it.
4. Imagine a finely ground diamond, one on your front, one on the back. The points of the diamonds nearly touch in the middle of your belly, leaving only a small gap between them.
5. Once those two diamonds are securely in place, place your palms on either side of your body.

6. Imagine two more diamonds in your palms. Their tips point towards the middle of your belly, like the other two diamonds, leaving a small space in the center between the four diamond tips.

7. Take a few deep breaths. When breathing out, direct your breath into the space between the four diamonds, as if fanning some flames.

8. Feel all four diamonds, standing strong, in the middle of your belly...

9. After a while, stand up from you sitting position and carefully move your body, still keeping the four diamonds in place.

10. The diamonds radiate out in all four directions... upwards and downwards...

11. See how their light is expanding outwards...

    How it fills the whole room around you...

    ... the whole city...

    ... the whole country...

    ... the whole planet...

    ... the whole universe...

Fan the flames in the center of your belly, between the four diamond tips, with your out-breath, and watch how your inner fire grows stronger and brighter and radiates out into the world...

Do this as long as you feel like it.

Tips:

1. The four diamonds exist beyond your imagination: they are very real energy patterns in your body!

2. The diamonds collect energies from the outside of your body and bring them into your body. During this process they transform energies that aren't life supportive into life supportive energies (transformation of negative into positive).

3. Over time you will feel your connection with the universe more and more clearly, and also your own place in the center of it! You will feel full of good Life-giving energy, stable and centered. You will recognise that everything that happens outside of you, happens within you.

By using this Power Tool you can take responsibility and consciously influence a positive energy balance in this world.

Super Powers

Welcome to the world of Super Powers. We all have Super Powers "on board" when we are born. But few of us develop them and work with them consciously. They mostly sit there, unused, and fade away – until we take the time to strengthen our "Super-muscles" and reactivate them again.

The following Power Tools will train your Super Powers. It will be very helpful, if you are already familiar with the Tools described on the previous pages. You need to be able to use your imagination and visualisation skills and to keep your concentration focused for quite a while. Otherwise you might get frustrated or simply won't be able to use your Super Powers at all – or at least not at will.

If you are a natural "dreamer" and find it easy to conjure up images, stories, smells, feelings in your mind and body, then you will be well set-up to train your Super Powers with the following Tools. If not, you can prepare yourself by practising your visualisation skills. Start with something simple like this: Imagine freshly baked bread... Smell it... See how crisp it is... Taste it...

In a next step, imagine your best friend, your favourite animal or place in every tiny detail... Engage as many of your senses as possible: what does he/she/it look like? What do you hear? His/her voice? Any other noises, sounds that you can hear when you think of the place or the person? How does it feel like, when you touch it/him/her? What smells do you notice?

Focus on the person, animal, place or object for as long as you can. When you get distracted and other "stuff" pops into your mind, take a few conscious breaths and gently bring yourself back to the image you want to focus on. Over time you will get more and more adept at conjuring up images at will and at keeping your attention focused on them.

On the next level play around with evoking feelings: joy, happiness, sadness, anger... Imagine a situation that makes you feel happy, for example. It can be a memory of something that you have experienced, or it can be something completely "new", something that you make up in your mind. Live the experience so totally as if it would happen right here and now. Try to feel and see every little nuance and detail within you. Let the feeling grow inside of you, until it fills you up completely. Allow yourself to express the feeling in whatever way comes up for you.

If you choose anger as your training ground, allow yourself to yell and scream and hit – a punching bag or a pillow (*not* your little sister or brother or dog or mum's precious vase – even if you feel like it!).

Side note: If you feel angry with somebody and need or want to get it out of your system, you might imagine him or her or the situation that makes you angry and let the anger out on a punching bag or pillow or mattress.

This kind of release often works wonders, and you will be able to address the actual situation and the person in a calmer and more centered way later on. Also try the Power Tools *Letting go I* and *Letting Go II* from the previous section if you feel overcome by strong feelings.

When you are able to conjure up images, situations and feelings within yourself at will, you will be well prepared to start practising your Super Powers.

All of the Tools in the following chapters open pathways to travel into different realities and to go beyond your usual everyday experiences. They also help you to shape your reality consciously and deliberately by entering "other worlds".

Please note: They are not always easy to handle – and even though some of us learn how to use them faster than others, it usually requires quite a bit of practise to apply them in a responsible and safe way.

Safety rules & protection gear

You will need some kind of safety belt or other protection gear to make sure you come back to your everyday reality safely and wholly.

- Always let somebody you trust know when you are experimenting with these Tools: they will be able to check on you if they don't hear from you after a long while.

- Choose a safe place for your practise: you want few people around – definitely not a public place. The more people around, the harder for you to feel and focus on your energies. The various energy fields and frequencies might interfere with your own and you might get distracted. This can be especially harmful when you have already entered a different reality: if you lose your focus at a crucial point during your journey into other realities, you might harm your Self or not find a safe way back.

- Use the protective Tools described in *Protection* to make sure that you don't lose your Self and that you come back safely into your body-mind-soul union.

- Please do not abuse or misuse your Super Powers! As they are powerful, the destructive effects would be even worse than with other Tools in this book. You might seriously harm your Self and others. Please take good care and use them wisely so that they will support you to shape your life and bring a lot of goodness to you (and others).

Beyond words – reading energy fields

all ages

Everything is energy vibrating at a certain frequency. The denser the energy field, the more condensed and visible it is as material body.

Every animal, including humans, can exchange information by reading each other's energy fields. How? By knowing their own energy field and its vibration and by "reading" the energy field of the other being. As said before, this used to be a natural and common form of communication amongst humans since ancient times. It was crucial for survival. In our modern world, humans rely more and more on other means to communicate: electronic devices like mobile phones, internet, social media and so on became a common form of information exchange, and humans in Western cultures mainly use words and numbers to get their information across. This is why our ability to read energy fields withered over the last few generations.

When we humans are born, we all come with the ability to read each other's energy fields. However, if we don't use it we lose it ☺

I will give you some examples to show you that you, too, have the ability to read energy fields and to communicate beyond words:

Have you ever thought of somebody whom you haven't met for a long time – and briefly afterwards he or she calls, or you see her/him in the streets? Have you ever entered a room and felt tension or a "bad atmosphere"? And then you learned afterwards that people in the room had had a heated conversation just before you came in? Or have you felt that something wasn't quite right with your friend even though she said, "I am fine"? The list goes on – and I am sure you can find many examples in your life where you read the energy field without being aware of it. We unconsciously do it all the time. It is hardwired in our system.

You can deliberately activate this form of communicating and exchanging information and use it at will and intentionally if you want to. It can be useful in many situations:

- to find out what's happening for others who might not be able to share their feelings and thoughts with you for various reasons.
- to communicate with other species (pets, wild animals, trees, stones,…).
- to communicate with people who don't want or cannot speak (babies, mute or autistic people, …).
- to exchange information with people who are far away – it saves you calling or messaging them, and you can directly link in with them in a much deeper and direct way.

Language can be quite a limiting tool. Often people are "lost for words" when things go really deep. We can use ESP (= Extra-Sensory Perception) and connect through linking directly into each other's energy field. By reading the other person's energy field we will "get the whole picture", not just snippets of information.

Humans might *say*, "I am fine" when clearly they are not. Animals *feel* what is really going on within us, and often come when people are sad: they can read the energy field and know something is up. This is why we so often feel deeply seen and understood by our companion animals. With this form of communication there are no socially or culturally accepted barriers – just pure clear information transfer.

1. First step is, that you become aware of your own energy field.

    How does it feel? This simple visualisation can help you to establish a stable base to begin with:

    Imagine a stream of light energy flowing from your heart to your belly center and back. A pulsating steady energy stream that connects your heart and the space below your belly button...

    It helps me to place my hands gently on my heart and my belly and to imagine the flow between those two places.

    Breathe deeply, and you might even feel a tingling sensation indicating the flow.

Do this regularly for a week or so – tune in during the day and think of the energy flow between your heart and your belly space.

By the way, you are not just imagining this flow: there is an actual energy exchange (which can be measured scientifically) happening all the time! However, it might help to use your imagination to become aware of it for the steps to come.

2. Are you able to quickly tune into your energy flow and are familiar with how "it" feels? You might see various colours of light, for example; your energy stream also has a very specific and unique "feel" to it – you will recognise it clearly the more you tune into it. Once you can clearly identify your own energy flow, you are ready to consciously connect with other energy fields. I say *consciously*, because in fact you are ALWAYS connected with other energy fields whether you think about it or not. What we are trying to establish here is that you deliberately link into them to send and receive information at will.

Feel your heart-belly energy stream.

Breathe deeply, and with the next outbreath imagine streaks of light branching out from your heart and belly... They grow and grow like tree branches... They form an energy circuit linking you with the land, the people, the animals, trees, plants... with the whole universe...

See how this light-mesh branches out from your belly-heart stream and connects you with everything else in the universe... Feel the pulsating of the energy flowing through the strands of this energy web...

It's great to do this every night before you go to sleep. It will not only help you with your ESP skills, it will also train your right brain hemisphere and open you up in preparation for many other useful skills that can support you a lot in your life. Keeping this energy flow and connection to a bigger energy web alive will bring a lot of Magic into your life. I won't say more – I am sure that you will feel and experience it for yourself.

3. The next step is to directly link into a specific energy field.

   Let's say you want to check in with your animal friend and see how he/she feels. Start with connecting to your heart-belly energy stream (see step 1.). Then branch out to your animal's energy field:

   Imagine an energy beam flowing from your heart-belly connection to the energy field of your animal friend. Watch how your energy beam connects to the energy field of the animal and merges with it...

   Next, ask a question and send a clear mind picture out to your animal friend, like a laser beam...

   Be specific and clear: instead of asking "how are you today?" (unclear, diffuse) you might want to ask "how is your body feeling today?", or even more specific: "how is your leg today?" (If there has been a leg injury, for example.)

Energy follows our thoughts: whenever we think of something we create an energy signal.

Imagine this signal travelling through the energy channel that leads from your heart-belly stream to your animal friend. Send out a clear and precise image.

It might take a bit of practice – over time your signals will become clearer and stronger and will be picked up by the other being faster and more concise.

Breathe deeply and let go... Open up and "listen"... Simply observe what's "popping up"...

The response to your signal might come immediately or, sometimes, it might take some time. It is important that you trust yourself. You might get a feeling of something. An image or thought might pop up. It might seem that it has nothing to do with your question. It doesn't matter. Simply notice what "comes up". You can make sense of it (using your mind and intuition) at a later stage.

In my experience, animals often respond in ways that are not necessarily related to our human ways of thinking and perceiving the world – after all they are not humans.

1. Once you feel there is nothing more coming from "the other end", you can either ask another question or clarify the first one. However, I often find that animals might not repeat their message and send another signal if you ask the same question twice, just to confirm. Stick with what you have got in the first place – and know that over time you will become

more and more fluent at sending and receiving energy signals and reading other energy fields.

On the following pages you will learn more about:

- telepathy – receiving messages on an intuitive level

- mind reading – using imagination and visualisation to send and receive messages

- ESP – opening your senses and linking into other energy fields to exchange information

Tips:

1. Be with Trees often. Sit with them, lie under them, walk in the forest... Trees expand your ability to read energy fields. They are true masters in this area and their energy will link into your "energy system", strengthen it and open it up.

2. Practice with your animal companions, close friends, little babies and toddlers. Animals, babies and little people are already well connected and pretty good at reading energy fields and receiving your signals so they can help you with your practice.

You can also use the "love connection" that connects you with close friends, for example. Your energy signals will travel along the "love energy stream" that already connects you strongly with the energy field of the other being. That is why we often *feel* when somebody we love is thinking of us.

Birds are great training partners as well.

Telepathy

age 8+

Want to practice your telepathic skills like Batman or X-man, Moondragon or Franklin Richards from the Fantastic Four?

Telepathy can be a very powerful and useful Tool, especially when you want to communicate with people who are far away from you and you can't just call or skype them for various reasons. Or if you want to communicate with other species, not just with humans.

Superheroes and Heroines in stories often use this Tool to outsmart each other or to save the world. As with all Tools: it is your responsibility to use it wisely and to the benefit of all, not only to increase your own power ☺

What is telepathy[4]? In short, you could describe it as receiving and sending information from one mind to another. It is a form of communication that our forefathers have used since ancient times. Animals use it as well to navigate their worlds.

You can communicate with others in many ways. The most common form we use is sound: we talk to each other. Humans in modern societies use words and numbers to share information with each other. We created technical devices that enable us to speak with somebody that lives at the other end of the world via skype or phone.

How did our forefathers do this, in a world without mobile phones, internet, TV and radio? Different indigenous tribes and family groups in Australia, for example, regularly gathered for meetings or to share important information. Living in the desert, without telecommunication, how did they know when and where to meet? How did they know when someone died or needed help? How did they stay in touch?

Sometimes, they communicated with physical signs that they left behind: cairns, paintings on rock walls, carvings in tree trunks. Sometimes, they sent messengers. However, these physical communication pathways were rather slow. So how did they transmit important information that needed to be shared immediately? The answer is: by sending thought messages. They were pretty good at it, and could "tune into each other" to exchange messages.

Have you ever thought about somebody very intensely and – "out of the blue" – this person called you or you met him or her in the street? Indigenous peoples have cultivated their ability to stay in touch with each other in this way since ancient times. They had and have people amongst them who are specialised in telepathic communication, like we have IT specialists in our modern human societies. Telepathy comes from the Greek words *tele* = "at a distance" and *pathy* = "touch, sensing". Some also call this communication form "extra-sensory perception" (ESP). No matter what we call it: we humans have the innate ability to sense each other, and if we practise we can use this ability to communicate with each other (and other beings) without speaking to them in words and numbers.

As said before, animals are fluent and very adept in this communication form. They are great teachers and practise companions. If you practise your telepathic or extra-sensory communication skills, you will be able to communicate with animals, with friends and family that are away (or "out of reception" because of various reasons), with people you want to connect to but haven't got their telephone number or contact details... the possibilities are infinite.

From my observation, a mutual "conversation" works best, when both or all partners are already connected through an emotional bond. That's usually the case with family members or friends. Love is a strong connector: if you love somebody or something, the information will flow easily and without interruption, because your whole being is more open towards them than with somebody who you don't know or like. If you don't have a special bond with the being or object, the communication flow depends more on your ability to focus and concentrate. The better you are in focusing your mental energy (thoughts, for example), the clearer you can visualise what you want to transmit, the stronger your message signal will be and the more direct it will reach the other being(s).

1. Practising visualisation skills & sending messages

Most likely, you do this all the time without noticing: whenever you imagine stories in your head, whenever you play with imaginary friends, whenever you think of how something will be (your next birthday party, for example), whenever you are hungry and dream of your favourite food, that yummy crunchy deliciously smelling pizza... you always use your imagination and visualisation skills.

We are all good at visualising, it is a natural innate Power Tool that we have all on board when we enter the physical world. We are using it all the time – mostly without being aware of it.

A good starting point to learn how to use this Tool consciously is your focus, your ability to deliberately steer your thought energy. Imagine your thoughts like rays of light: the more you are able to bundle them together and focus them on one point, the sharper and stronger the light will be in this one point, like a laser beam. The better you are able to focus your mental energy on one point (an image, thought, message), the clearer the message (energy signal) you are sending out will be.

As said before, animal friends are great practise partners as they are already tuned in and familiar with this communication form. They react immediately, when you "get it right" and when your thought beam is strong and steady. I practised a lot with my horse friends. It is an amazing feeling to ride horses entirely with "mind aides" – without bridles and other external controls.

If you don't have any animal friends, practise with family members or close friends – someone with whom you have a loving and trusting relationship. That will help to keep the reception channels open between you and the other person.

Take some deep breaths and relax.

If you want, close your eyes... It might help you to stay focused and not get distracted...

Become aware of your surroundings... sounds... smells...

Feel your body, feel how alive you are...

Call up a picture of the animal/friend in your mind...

Ask the animal/person if they are open to talk to you... wait for a "yes"- or a "no"-feeling...

If you get a "yes", send your animal or human friend a message.

Examples:

Imagine yourself going for a walk with your dog – picture yourself how you walk along the road, through the streets, in the park, along the beach... After a bit of practice you will be able to send out a clear image, and your dog will come running in no time without you having to call! Or think of your best friend and ask him/her to get in touch with you. Be open to what form (s)he might choose – (s)he might call or just pop in or tell you the next day that (s)he had thought of you intensely... You might also receive a mind message from her/him in return!

If you want, ask an open question like "How are you?" or "What is going on in your life?" Then wait for the answer. Be patient and allow time.

Over time, you will be able to receive messages increasingly fast and clear. Important is, that you breathe and keep yourself still like a lake in calm weather. You can only see to the ground if the surface is still and smooth.

Experiment and play around with this Power Tool. You will get better and better the more you use it.

2. Receiving messages

After some time, you will realise that you will be able to easily send messages to your animal and human friends and family. And you might even be able to receive their messages!

From my experience, it can take a while until we are able to receive messages clearly. Especially, if we are big thinkers and our mind is very active. No matter what type of person you are, just keep playing with this Tool and allow yourself all the time you need. Most people eventually learn to speak their mother language when they are little, some sooner, some later. The same is true for your telepathic language skills.

Tips:

1. We all use this Power Tool a lot without noticing. To use it consciously can be quite handy when you
   - want to exchange messages with other species.
   - want to get in touch with people immediately and cannot reach them by phone or via the internet.

2. It's also a lot of fun and you will be surprised how easy it will flow with a little practice.

   I often use it to call our animal friends, so that I don't have to run around and look for them. I also use it with my son Noa when he is outside and I cannot see him and I want to let him know that dinner is ready ☺

3. This Power Tool allows you to enter the first (basic) level of extrasensory perception (ESP). There is much more to learn and experience, and if you are interested, you can go deeper. As said before, people use and experiment with various forms of ESP such as remote viewing and mind reading since ancient times.

   You will find more resources online, or better: within yourself. The many different views on this topic "out there" can be quite confusing. As these forms of communication are hardwired in an ancient part of your Self, you can always access them within. Use your power center (see *Diamond Power Station*) and trust your intuition, your tuition from within.

Read my mind

age 10+

What would happen if we could read people's minds?

Imagine picking up all the "stuff" that people around you are thinking! Negative things included...

What if...

I often wish people could read my mind. Then I wouldn't have to use so many words to explain things, but could just beam thoughts and images into people's heads. I have experienced something like that when swimming with dolphins and whales in the wild. They are able to send and receive holographic mind pictures: they beamed images of how they perceive their world into my head and could read my emotional, mental and physical state perfectly. One day, I went for a swim in the Ocean and my knee started to hurt. When I tuned into my body, a picture of my knee "popped up" in my mind, and I saw a very tight, very red muscle string. All of a sudden a single dolphin approached me and pointed his beak towards my knee, sending out a series of clicks and other sounds. I felt a tingling and vibration in my knee – and in my mind I saw how the muscle relaxed and changed colour. When the dolphin swam away after a few seconds, my knee felt completely fine again.

If you have an animal companion you might know that they read your mood and usually want to help you.

Your dog might come and put her head in your lap when you are sad, for example. Horses, dogs, cats, birds – all animals can "read your mind" and pick up the emotional and mental state you are in. We humans can do this, too! Newborn babies are very good mind readers. They sometimes cry "out of the blue" when they pick up negative energies in their environment. As we grow up, we focus more on developing other senses: hearing and seeing things, touching things, tasting things... And as a consequence, we lose our mind reading and "energy sensing" abilities. However, this doesn't mean we cannot do it anymore. It simply means we need to exercise our "mind reading muscles" so that they become strong and function again.

Some people ban Super Powers into the land of mysticism and fantasy. If we want to de-mystify mind-reading, we can look at it through a scientific lens: "Our brain works off electrical activity, a bit like a computer", says Stephen Sigurnjak, senior lecturer in electronics at the University of Central Lancashire. When we concentrate on something, neurons are transmitting electric impulses in the brain. These impulses or brainwaves can be received and "read" by others. Scientists and inventors are using this knowledge to create mind-powered products. They came up with some pretty amazing inventions:

Cars of some scalextric (car racing game) are powered by the players' mind-powers: the higher their concentration levels the faster the cars. BMW modified a real car (BMW i3) so that it can be driven remotely just using a person's thoughts. Find some more examples in the *Appendix*.

1. Sending mind-messages

Usually, sending out messages is easier for most people than receiving them. In order to send out mind-messages, simply concentrate and hold an image of your message in your thoughts. Replay this image or a whole sequence of images (like a film clip) for a while, until you feel the message has been transmitted.

You can practise this with a friend or a family member. Just be aware: if they are not so good at receiving messages (yet), they might not "get it". As said before animals are excellent mind readers, so they are great teachers and training partners. They instantly show a reaction. Start with sending out simple messages like "Look at me". Babies in the first couple of months of their life are good training partners, too.

2. Receiving mind-messages

In order to be able to receive messages, you need to "clear your mind" of your own thoughts. You can only write something on a page once it's blank, right? Otherwise you wouldn't be able to read the message, as it would be all mixed up with words or images that are already on there.

Clearing you mind is easier said than done. Meditation practitioners and yoga masters are sometimes practising for years, before they can still their minds. I encourage you to regularly practice *Breathing with the River* and to calm your mind and body through exercises like *Letting go I* and *Letting Go II*. The more you do this, the easier it will become. *The Journey into your heart* is also a good preparation, before you use the following Tool.

1. Close your eyes... Breathe deeply a few times and imagine how all tensions... all thoughts... everything... flows out of you and deep into the earth...

2. Imagine you are a still ocean... stretching wide to the horizon...

3. Feel the power stream between your belly and your heart center...

4. See the energy web branching out from you, connecting you with your surroundings...

    Open yourself to the people and the possibilities around you...

    Feel everything...

    Sense how you are one with everything around you...

5. Now merge with the person/animal/being whose mind you want to read...

6. Breathe deeply... Open your eyes... Look at the person/animal/being...

    Look at them closely and examine them without thinking...

7. Now squint your eyes and let them wander through the space around the person/animal/being... Breathe... Relax... Get a feeling for what the person/animal/being is and what not.

8. Open yourself fully... and now look at the person/animal/being directly for 10-15 seconds, then quickly turn away. Close your eyes and visualise the face, eyes, shape... Notice what you *feel*...

   Breathe...

   Let the person's/animal's/being's thoughts fill your mind.

9. Interact with the person/animal/being by talking, playing, touching them (if you know them well and/or if it feels right) or sit in stillness. Whatever you feel like doing, you will receive thoughts, feelings, images, sounds in your head.

   Trust your feelings and instincts and allow your mind being flooded by the signals you receive.

Tips:

1. This Power Tool works best if you are very playful with it. Don't be uptight or try too hard. Relax and breathe and open yourself.

2. Don't analyse or doubt your feelings. Things will pop up in your mind, and you might be flooded with images and thoughts. Trust that they are not yours and simply stay open to receive them.

3. Be patient and gentle with yourself. It might take a while before you consciously can read the mind of others – or it might be really easy for you. It doesn't matter. Just keep playing with this Tool, and over time you will be able to read what's going on in others more and more clearly.

Shapeshifting

age 10+

Do you know the old fairy tale of the frog that shapeshifted into a handsome prince? Or a newer story in the Harry Potter series where Professor McGonagall transforms a desk into a pig in "Transfiguration class"? Well, you will find shapeshifters all around you in stories and movies, if you have a closer look. But is shapeshifting only found in the world of fiction and myth? Or does it happen in "the real world", too?

I want to answer this question from my own experience. I have seen an old woman turn into a deer in the forests of Montana. I have also seen a hawk turn into a Spirit Being in the plains of Usbekistan. And I have witnessed shapeshifting on some other occasions. Shapeshifting is an old magic Tool. It is not an "easy-to-use" Tool that everyone can handle. It requires practise and determination. Usually A LOT. I wouldn't recommend starting with this Tool if you haven't done any of the basic exercises in this book or are familiar with similar exercises, as you might get frustrated and dismiss that it even works.

Shapeshifters use the power of their imagination and their ability to focus to actually change their physical reality, sometimes within seconds. So you have to train your "concentration muscles". You need to be able to tame your monkeys (see *The Monkey Mind*) and to ride your wild horses (see *Letting go II*) in order to get anywhere with this Tool.

You can be anything you want!

Shapeshifting can be valuable to experience the world from a different perspective. Shamans use it to travel to places they can't access otherwise or to gain powers they don't have in their human form. Great navigators used to shapeshift into birds to orientate themselves from above. Hunters shapeshift into the animals they track to understand their moves and to intimately link into their ways of being. I have seen people deal with their fears by shapeshifting into another version of themselves that isn't afraid, scared or worried. I once shapeshifted into a mountain goat to overcome my fear of heights on a tricky and (for me) terrifying alpine track.

In this chapter you will find some *basic* exercises to hone your shapeshifting skills and to get used to this Power Tool. Even if you are a natural and have already experienced shapeshifting these exercises might still be useful to learn how to consciously focus and direct your energies at will.

Tool I

1. This Tool works best, when you are outdoors. A park or sports field is fine. Just make sure that you are undisturbed and not distracted.

2. Find a comfortable, quiet spot and sit or lie down. Begin with your usual pre-practise routine to center your Self. Breathe deeply, set your intention and your goal for this practise and call in your Spirit Helpers.

3. To explain how the Tool works, I will choose the following intention as an example – you can use it for your practise or choose your own intention and scenario: "I want the bird over there to come closer and sit right in front of me."

   Choose an exact spot where you want the bird to be. Of course, you have to make sure that a) there are any birds around, b) you choose a specific one and c) there aren't any circumstances that would prevent the bird from coming to you (for example, your dog lying in front of you or a cat in the tree next to you).

4. Close your eyes and imagine the bird flying towards you landing at exactly the spot you want it to land. Keep this image strongly in your head. Imagine every detail. See how the bird's wings flap up and down. See its beak, the colour of its tail feathers...

   Focus on the images and don't let them slip away. If they do, bring them back and hold them strong: see how the bird flies towards the spot in front of you.

Watch how it lands, the little head moving back and forth, eying you curiously...

Once you are able to hold these images strong and long enough, the bird will follow your lead – and when you open your eyes, you will see it sitting right there.

This Power Tool is great to strengthen your "concentration muscles" and to prepare you for shapeshifting.

Tool II

1. Go to a power place in nature. I find it easiest to practise outdoors. The more natural and "wilder" the surroundings the better. If you cannot go outdoors or haven't any natural environment nearby, find a place where you will be undisturbed for a while.

2. Choose something around you that you want to be.

3. Start with your usual pre-practise routine to center your Self. Breathe deeply, set your intention (for example: "I want to shapeshift into this tree") and call in your Spirit Helpers.

4. To describe this Tool I use the example of a tree, as trees are easy to find, but you can choose whatever you like, of course.

Choose a tree and examine it with all your senses: look at its shape, feel the bark and the leaves, wrap your arms around it and look up into the branches...

Smell, hear, listen... and observe as many details as possible.

Spend as much time to get to know the tree as you need and want to. You might even decide to come back another time to continue your practise.

5. Once you feel ready, sit down with your back touching the tree.

   You don't necessarily have to touch the being or object you choose for your shapeshifting-practise. In my experience, being as close as possible makes it easier to use this Tool in the beginning, though.

6. Breathe deeply and close your eyes. Feel yourself merging with the tree. Your back expands into the bark... Roots grow out of your feet, deep down into the Earth...

   Feel how – with every breath – your whole body becomes one with the tree... until you *are* the tree...

7. Keep breathing and stay the tree for a while. Feel the world as Tree...

8. Come back slowly into your body. Open your eyes, and gently massage your arms, legs and feet. You can also tap with your fingers along your arms, legs, on the top of your head and around the heart to bring your awareness and energies back into your human shape. Finally, stretch and slowly get up.

It can be a good idea to have a drink of water and/or eat something to ground your Self.

If you feel dizzy, you should shorten your practise and shapeshift back earlier the next time. If you didn't shapeshift for long and still feel unwell, then it is best to ask a person you trust or your Spirit Helpers for advice (if you have established a clear way of communicating with them and know how to receive their messages). Shapeshifting might not be the "right" thing for you at this moment in time!

Tool III

1. Start with your usual pre-practise routine to center your Self. Breathe deeply, set your intention and call in your Spirit Helpers.

2. Close your eyes and call up a clear image of what you want to be. I find it easiest to start with something I am familiar with. This can be a dog, a tree in the garden, a river, bird...

   Focus on the image. Look at every detail... colour, shape, texture... What does it feel like when you touch it? How does it smell? Bring the whole image to life.

3. Hold the image as vividly as you can. Breathe deeply and see yourself changing. Feel how your skin changes and becomes the bark of a tree, the fur of a dog or whatever it is that you want to be. Feel how your toes grow into roots, and your arm into branches...

Keep breathing and focusing on the image, while you see and feel your Self shapeshifting into another life form...

4. Some people find it helpful to behave like the being or object they want to become. This is why you can see shamans perform ceremonial dances, wearing huge Eagle wings, making bird noises. The dance and drumming or rattling brings them into a trance (see *Trance – Portal to the Otherworld*), the energy of the Eagle feathers and imitating the noises and movements of the big bird allow them to merge with Eagle energies – until they will shapeshift into an eagle if they choose to.

Experiment with various ways and find out what works best for you. Shapeshifting can be quite an amazing experience – enjoy!

5. When you are ready, breathe deeply and consciously, and slowly come back into your human body... Allow time!

   Open your eyes and stretch your legs and arms gently. Open your mouth wide as if yawning and slowly circle your head. Keep breathing deeply into your belly and touch the ground until you feel fully "back" in your human shape. Eating and drinking will help you as well to come back into your body.

Tips:

1. This is a Power Tool for advanced learners! Make sure you have an anchor point in your everyday reality to ensure that you "come back" safely. Also ask your Spirit Helpers to call you back in time.

2. I highly recommend that you tell somebody whom you trust about what you are doing. Get them to check on you after a while. They do not have to interrupt your practise, but can check in from a distance.

3. Shapeshifting takes a lot of energy. You might feel dizzy or nauseous. You might even have a light headache after you shapeshifted back. Observe yourself closely: If you feel unwell at any one point during the exercise, stop immediately and shapeshift back to your human form.

4. Some people feel so comfortable and great in another shape that they do not necessarily want to shapeshift back. I once shifted into an albatross and enjoyed myself and the feeling of surfing in the wind so much that I "completely forgot" my human reality and ignored the voices of my Spirit Guides who tried to call me back. Luckily, my shaman teacher, the old woman I mentioned above who transformed into a deer, came and brought me back: she emptied a bucket with ice-cold river water over my head. My whole body ached and I felt dizzy for about two days afterwards (not because of the icy water!).

I don't tell you this to scare you. I just want to let you know that this Power Tool needs to be treated with some caution and respect.

The Art of Disappearing

age 10+

Do you sometimes wish you were invisible? Especially when your mum has thousands of jobs for you to do – or when you have to go to school in the mornings?

Well, I won't encourage you to use this Power Tool to not be helpful or to sneakily "get away" with things. As with all Power Tools, it doesn't work that well for you if your intention isn't clear and life-supportive. Why? Because it will literally backfire, if you use a Tool in a way that causes trouble. We are all part of one big body of life. We are not separate individual beings – even though we often think we are. We are like different cells forming one body. Each cell has its own individual membrane and its own function to guarantee the wellbeing of the whole body. And yet all cells are interconnected.

Ideally, they all work together to assure that the whole body is in balance. If one group of cells gets out of hand, which happens, for example, when cancer cells grow exuberantly, they tip the balance – and affect the whole body (dis-ease).

Keep this in mind and heart when you practice your disappearing skills – or when using any other Power Tools for that matter ☺

Background information

Some, if not all Power Tools, developed out of a necessity. The Art of Disappearing was needed to survive, and still is for some species. Predators needed to be invisible in order to be hidden from prey. And prey animals that had the ability to "disappear" would, of course, live longer.

The Art of Disappearing is deeply ingrained in the story of us humans as well. We find it in fairy tales, myths and legends, in war history and in all shamanic traditions. Becoming invisible is one of the treasured Super Powers of Super Heroes. It is a very useful skill to have when it comes down to two basic factors in our life: the scramble for food and power. This is the main reason why it became so popular. Humans also abused and misused this art form many times to kill, hunt and overpower other life forms.

Tool I

1. Set a clear intention.
2. Breathe deeply to relax your whole Body-Mind-Soul system. If you need to, use other Tools to balance your Self (for example: *Letting go I*).
3. When you feel calm and comfortable within your Self, close your eyes and do the following: with your next

in-breath imagine how you draw your energy into your body – suck all the energy that is radiating out from you deep into your belly center.

Imagine the energy forming a ball that gets smaller and smaller within your belly center... until you cannot see it anymore.

4. Keep focusing on the point where the energy ball disappeared.

Tip:

In the beginning, you might only be able to hold your energy in for a short while. That's fine. Over time, without you noticing, you will be able to hold your focus for longer and longer periods of time.

The more you are able to "suck your energies in", to hold them there and see them "disappear", the less you will be visible to other beings. Your energy won't disappear completely, of course, but by drawing it in and holding it there you won't be visible to others.

Tool II

1. Set a clear intention.
2. Breathe deeply to relax your whole Body-Mind-Soul system. If you need to, use other Tools to balance your Self (for example: *Letting go I*).
3. Close your eyes and perceive everything within and around you with all your senses. Listen to the

sounds... Feel the warmth/cold/wind/sun... Smell the freshness/staleness/smells in the air...

4. Take some deep breaths and imagine how the energy field that makes up your body expands and slowly merges with your surroundings... Imagine that your body is dissolving and commingling with everything that is around you...

Let your energies flow freely and keep "commingling"...

Tip:

As you practice using these Power Tools, you will experience that others won't notice you anymore. You will literally become invisible, not only to fellow humans, but also to animals.

I once was practising in the forest, sitting with my back against a tree trunk. I was completely "gone" and felt at one with my surroundings, "dissolving" my Self more and more. When I finally opened my eyes, there were three deer grazing about two meters next to me. They were as startled to see me as I was. As long as I had been commingling with my surroundings, they hadn't noticed me!

Tool III - the invisible cloak

1. Set a clear intention.
2. Breathe deeply to relax your whole body-mind-soul. If you need to, use other Tools to balance your Self.

3. Imagine an energy shield of light forming around you. Watch what happens...

   My shield sometimes appears in different colours. Often it is bright white. At other times it is of a pulsating blueish colour. Some people I have spoken to describe a warm golden colour. Just be with whatever shows up for you.

4. Once the first layer of the shield is up, go round and round again and wrap light-layer after light-layer around your physical body. Stop when you feel the shield is strong and impenetrable enough.

Tips:

1. The functioning of this Tool depends to a great degree on your ability to build up a strong shield. Set your intention and trust that your Spirit Helpers will support you to hold the shield in place for as long as you need it to be.

2. Don't doubt! Doubts or worries often tear holes in our energy field. When they come up either stop them – be determined and strong – or put the Power Tool you are using aside and deal with your fear(s) first. You can do this on your own, but it often is helpful to seek support. Connect with your Spirit Guide(s) (also see *Meet your Spirit Guide*) or ask a person you trust for help.

3. Remember to take your invisibility cloak off!

I once practiced at a beach. I had arranged to meet some friends afterwards. They were supposed to pick me up in their car. When I came to the place where we wanted to meet they weren't there yet. As I didn't want to wait, I decided to walk along the roadside. There was only one direction they could come from as the road led down to the beach and back into town. After a short while I saw their car in the distance – I was sure they would see me (there was nobody else around and I was walking on a grassy stretch right beside the road). So I was a little surprised when they didn't stop. I assumed that they had decided to drive a little further to turn their car around more comfortably and would come back to pick me up. So I continued walking. After a short while my friends drove by again, this time heading into town. They didn't stop to pick me up, they didn't even slow down. Where they trying to be funny? I was walking right next to the road. Surely they must have seen me! This was when I suddenly remembered my beach practise and my "invisible cloak". I quickly "took it off" and waved my hands frantically. Luckily, one of them saw me in the rear mirror. They stopped and came back. To this day we tell this story when we see each other: They passed me twice and still swear that there was nobody there. They hadn't seen me, even though they had looked out for me – and there had been nowhere to hide! No trees, no bushes, no big boulders...

So remember this story when you practise the Art of Disappearing ☺

Transfiguration

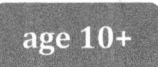

We humans are part of a bigger whole: we are part of the Earth body which in turn is part of the Milky Way Galaxy which in turn is part of a whole lot of other galaxies... Let's focus on our living planet Earth for now: we are just one little part of the whole Earth body that consists of many other life forms with various shapes and functions. Let's say humans are the fingers of the body. We consist of the same building blocks as other life forms on this planet. And we are connected to all the other parts through skin/cell tissue and blood vessels. Together we form one body. If something happens to us, let's say a cut, this affects the whole body.

As you can observe around you, a lot of "modern" humans aren't aware of their close connection to the whole Earth body and their impact on the whole system. They see themselves as separate little units and act as if they can control life of the whole system. We cannot: our actions or non-actions certainly have an influence on Life on this planet as a whole, but to think we can control Life on planet Earth is overestimating our powers.

I leave it up to you to ponder our position and influence as humans in the worldwide Web of Life. It certainly changed quite a lot over time. I would like to bring your attention to *your* power as a little cell or part of a little cell. On your journey through this book you might have discovered many of your special powers. You might have felt your connection to and your place within this web of life. If one pulls one string in a web, it can be felt throughout the web. Even the slightest of movements has an effect. As an integral inseparable part of the web you have great power as your actions will influence all other cells in the body.

In this chapter I will show you another ancient Tool that you can use on your own or in a group. The more people use it at the same time, the more impact it will have. However, using it on your own already makes a huge difference.

Use this Tool to bring balance wherever you see it is needed. I will focus on balancing Land (skin) and Water Ways (blood vessels) here. You can, of course, expand it and apply it to any other body parts of Mother Earth including Humans.

1. Before you begin, choose a topic. Let's say you want to support a river near you that is affected by pollution. Or you want to help re-balance land where humans have cut down trees.

2. Breathe deeply into your belly, center yourself, set your intention and call in your Spirit Helpers.

3. Tune into your *Diamond Power Station*. Breathe into the center between the Diamonds and see the energy pulsating...

4. When the energy is strong and steady, let it radiate out and direct it towards the land/river/lake/ocean or whatever it is you want to balance. Watch how the bright steady flow of energy floats like a blanket over the land/river/lake/ocean. Let it expand until it completely covers the affected area.

5. Take a few deep breaths... Imagine how all the things that destroy the balance are sucked into the energy blanket. The blanket is like a big cleaning cloth that absorbs all the destructive energies and substances...

Watch how all the things that hinder balance are sucked up into your energy blanket...

You might notice a change of colour or brightness in the energy blanket. That's ok. Keep sending out bright energy from your diamonds into the blanket and watch how the energies that come from the land/river/Lake/ocean dissolve into the blanket and are transformed into bright white energy.

6. Keep breathing and wait until the blanket is completely pure and bright again.

7. When you feel the process is finished, take another deep breath and blow on the energy in your Diamond Power Center. See how the energy flares up like a fire. Once your energy fire is going strong, send pulsating energy out into the blanket and let it flow from there into the land/river/lake/ocean like rain falling from a blanket of clouds.

Watch how the bright energy from your Diamond Power Center seeps into the land/river/lake/ocean, nurturing it...

Do this for as long as it feels right.

8. Once you feel it is time to stop, gently pull back your energy into your center. Watch until the energy blanket has dissolved into thin air. Thank your Self and your Spirit Helpers.

You can repeat this process as often as you like. If you do it in a group together with others, the transfiguration process will be even stronger and often faster which can be helpful, for example in heavily polluted areas.

Tips:

1. Allow time for the transfiguration process to happen. It might take a while. Just keep breathing and send bright energy from your Diamond Power Center.

2. Some people use sound to assist the transfiguration process. They sing the unwanted energy out of the land/river/lake/ocean and sing balancing energies into it in return. You can experiment with this and see if it helps you to focus and direct your energies. You can use whatever song comes up for you (it can be any sounds, tones, mantras, chants etc.) – important is that it supports your visualisation, flows easily and strengthens your concentration.

3. Transfiguration processes also work with words. If you use prayers and affirmations in your everyday life, you might want to use words to assist the energy transfiguration. "I draw pure Life energy from my Diamond Power Center into a blanket of Light. Let everything that doesn't serve balance be transformed..." and so on. Make up your own "prayers" or use powerful ones that you already know. Don't think – just use what comes up naturally. And only if it helps you. I personally prefer stillness to focus on the process. Find out what works best for *you*.

Teleportation

age 12+

You find the prefix *tele* in many words: *tele*vision, *tele*phone, *tele*gram, *tele*graph, *tele*pathy... *Tele* comes from the Greek words telos = "end, completion" and teleios = "perfected". Its usual meaning is "at a distance" or "from afar". With a television set you can view things that are happening far from you, in other parts of the world. A telephone allows you to speak with people who are far away. Telepathy, as you have seen in *Super Powers I*, is the art of exchanging messages using thought energy. You might already guess what teleportation is all about! It is the skill to move (lat. portare = "to carry") things or your Self from A to B by directing energy instead of travelling the actual distance between A and B.

This Power Tool is examined in quantum mechanics (energy and particle teleportation), and more and more scientists are fascinated by its possibilities. It is another ancient Tool that has been used for thousands of years and is still known and used by some humans.

This Tool is not a "beginner's Tool" and requires a lot of determination, commitment and perseverance. If you wanted to climb Mt Everest, you would need to practise and exercise your body for a long time, continuously and regularly, before you would be able to start your climb. It is no different here. Only continuous efforts will train your Mind-Body-Spirit enough to be able to use some of the more advanced Power Tools described here. In this book you will learn *the basics* to start your training.

Please don't try to teleport your physical Self just yet! This takes *a lot* of practice, and you need to learn how to disassemble and re-assemble your energy field – which is quite a task! People have died, because they weren't able to do this properly. So, please, start with moving energy and small objects! This is fun and will train your ability to feel and deliberately move energy within and around you.

Tool I

(visual teleportation exercise)

1. Find a quiet place and start with your usual pre-practise routine: center your Self, set a clear intention and call in your Spirit Helpers.

2. Close your eyes and feel the core energy in your belly center that radiates out from your body like rays from the sun. See how this energy field pulsates gently, sending out light waves...

   Take a couple of deep breaths, and with each out-breath imagine how you fan the field like a fire, making it more and more powerful... When you feel your energy field bright and strong, imagine an object in front of you...

Feel your energy field... then *feel* the energy field of the object...

3. Imagine how your energy field and the energy field of the object are commingling. They blend together like two pots of paint flowing into each other...

4. See and *feel* how the energy of the object disappears and leaves the space in front of you...

5. Then concentrate on a spot a short distance away from you... Imagine every detail of it... Breathe deeply, and with the next out-breath see and *feel* how the energy of the object materialises at the new place...

6. Try and hold the object there for a while before you retract your energy field... Once you feel ready, slowly open your eyes, breathe deeply and come back to the "outside world".

Tool II

(You need someone to practise with.)

1. Find someone who would like to be your "guinea pig". Don't worry: it will be fun for both of you. Tell your partner it is a magic trick, which, in a way, it is. Choose a quiet place and center your Self with a couple of deep breaths, set a clear intention and call in your Spirit Helpers.

2. Close your eyes and hold your hands out in front of you, about your body width apart. Feel the energy flowing between your palms...

   You can slowly increase and decrease the distance between your palms, like sea grass in a current, to strengthen the feeling.

3. Now bring your hands together and knead all the energy into a tight ball.

   You might feel a tingling in your palms...

4. Once you have a nice compact energy ball in front of your belly hold it there for a couple of breaths. With each out-breath imagine yourself fanning the field like a fire, making it more and more powerful... When you *feel* your energy field bright and strong, open your eyes. Keep your focus on the energy ball between your hands.

5. Ask your partner to hold out his/her hands, a body width apart, like you did in the beginning.

6. Focus on the energy ball and feel how the energy ball moves from your hands to the hands of your partner. *Feel* the movement!

7. If all went well, your partner will feel the energy ball you teleported.

   Be patient – give your Self time. You will need to train your concentration muscles big time to send energy (and at a later stage objects) from one place to another.

Tool III

(physical teleportation exercise)

Once you have mastered the first two Tools, you can start practising with material objects. Use small and light objects to start of with as this is easier. I practise with a tiny gemstone.

1. Find a quiet place and start with your usual pre-practise routine: center your Self, set a clear intention and call in your Spirit Helpers.

2. Breathe deeply and close your eyes. Hold the object in your hands in front of your belly. Make sure you are in a comfortable relaxed position.

    Tune into the energy field of the object. *Feel* it... If you want, spark the energy field with your breath.

3. Now feel how the energy field of your body merges with the energy of the object. Feel how the two energies in your hands blend into each other, mixing like two liquids.

    You might feel a tingling or warm sensation.

4. Focus on the commingling of your energy with the energy of the object... *Feel* the energy of the object... its flow... its essence... mixing with your energy. *Feel* the power of the combined energies in your hands...

5. Keep breathing, and with your next out-breath let the object disappear from your hands. Feel how its energy moves to a nearby spot. Feel how it is moved by the

power of the combined energy fields. Once you can feel it at the destination, slowly retract your energy: watch how the two energy fields separate again. *Feel the object firmly and defined at its new spot.*

6. Open your eyes – and see the object appear at its new spot.

Tips:

1. Use your visualisation skills in the beginning to support you. However, after a while you will notice that you *actually move* energies and material objects and not "just" thought energy.

2. Keep playing! Don't expect instant results. This doesn't mean that it is not possible to have instant results! However, in my experience, these Tools require a lot of practise – sometimes many years of regular continuous training –, before you will actually be able to apply them.

3. Please remember: these Tools will give you a basic foundation and a glimpse into the world of teleportation and other Super Powers. If you are really committed and interested in exploring this field in more depths, there are specific ways to move on from visual to material teleportation (= when you teleport material objects, including yourself).

Material teleportation is like a master course, and I highly recommend an experienced teacher at your side if you want to explore this further. Teleportation on a physical level requires that you know how to ground and unground your Self (your energy field) and that you are able to *easily* perform the exercises in this book. Otherwise, you might get lost in "pure energy realms" and not re-connect with your physical reality.

Trance – portal to the Otherworld

age 12+

We need to lose our mind in order to be able to enter other realities. The mind is a control freak and often blocks access to the "unknown": to Dream- and Spirit World and other realms of Life-Magic – simply because it can and because it wants things to make sense according to the programs that are already installed on its hard drive. This is why the mind often rejects and dismisses "Magic". It doubts, worries, is scared.

In the previous chapters you got some Tools to calm your mind, your thoughts. Trance is another very powerful Tool that bypasses the mind and opens the door to other realities. It is widely applied – and I am sure you have used it before without realising it. Have you ever turned the music up and totally "lost" your Self? Or "zoned out" completely while playing your drum kit? Have you ever been so engrossed in a book or a movie that you weren't aware of your surroundings anymore? These are all states of trance. Some people enter trance states when hiking in the mountains or running marathons. Repetitive work on an assembly line can also lead to trance-like states of mind, and military studies have shown that military marches and the marching of soldiers are able to induce a trance.

There are many, many different ways and Tools to enter trance. I could write a whole book just about this topic. Below I will share two basic toolboxes for you to experiment with – as mentioned before: using the Tools in this book will get you *started* on your Path of Power – the rest will follow. Trust your journey ☺

Some background information

Trance is important for our balance and healthy functioning. It is a state of deep relaxation when our mind is still and focused at the same time. This is when the portal to "other realities" opens... When the boundaries between "inside and outside" blur and our intuition speaks loud and clear. Out of a trance often emerge strong visions, ideas for a project, new creations, healing and self-created rituals.

People have used and use steady rhythms in music, song and dance since thousands of years to walk through the portals and to enter other states of consciousness. They use rhythms and sounds to heal, to communicate with "God" or Higher Powers, to find guidance and advice and answers to their questions, and to travel into other realities like Spirit or Dreamworld. Trance is a platform for ceremony and ritual opening the door for Magic to happen. In short: Whenever you want to shift your reality and enter a different "state of mind", the Power Tools in this chapter will be a great vehicle to get you there.

Safety tips

1. Be aware of the people around you, when you experiment with these Tools. It is great to have fun at a dance party and "zone out" for a bit. However, if you enter a deep trance state you need to take good care – of your Self and others – and make sure everybody is safe. When practising these Tools, you will soon experience that it makes a huge difference whether you use them in a party atmosphere or during a ceremony, for example.

   Trust your intuition and feelings, make sure you are in a safe environment, with well-balanced people or alone (remember your safety belt: always tell somebody that you are practising), and with no harmful objects around you.

2. Make sure you have some grounding techniques to "call you back".

   When you begin practising with these Tools, I highly recommend that you involve an experienced person whom you trust to supervise you. Even though I "only" show you the beginning stages of trance work, this are powerful Tools that could potentially cause troubles if you "get stuck" or lose your Self in a trance.

3. Observe your Self.

   When I started practising and experimenting with trance many years ago, I often found that I didn't want to come back into my "normal state of mind". I am a dreamer and I loved the trance state so much that I wanted to stay there. If you notice a similar reaction within your Self, be careful not to overdo it ☺ It is great to be able to roam Dreamspace and Otherworld and to go beyond our physical everyday reality. However: in my view, we are here in our bodies to experience "physical reality" in all its forms and shapes. We can get support, guidance and advice from other realities, and this will help us tremendously when navigating the ups and downs of our physical journey. Losing ourselves in other worlds is not what we came here for, though.

4. Breathing

   Your breath is an essential Tool to navigate through your life with ease and to enter other realities. Panting like a dog is an age-old method to access trance state: some call it hyperventilation. Dogs are masters at panting – their secret is to take very shallow breaths, but please start with other, gentler breathing techniques! Hyperventilation can have serious side effects such as dizziness, tingling in lips, hands or feet, headache, nausea, fainting. Please don't take this lightly. Any reactions of your body are STOP signs that need to be taken seriously.

Having said all this, deep accentuated belly breaths can support you to enter a balanced trance state. Use the breathing exercises described in *Code of practise* in step 2 to center and prepare your Self *before* using the Tools in this chapter. Try to keep your breathing rhythm steady and aligned with the rhythm of the music or your movements (Toolbox 1), or adopt a steady calm breathing rhythm (Toolbox 2).

Observe your Self. How do you need to breathe to enter trance state?

Don't try too hard: Let things flow easily and naturally.

Toolbox I – Trance induced by external triggers

Every energy wave has a rhythm. Every life form has its own innate rhythm. Our heartbeat follows a rhythm. This is why humans love playing music, dancing and singing. Fast, up-beat rhythms bring our life energies in motion. Slow steady rhythms have a grounding and calming effect.

Steady repetitive rhythms affect our brain and help us to enter a world beyond our usual everyday life. It is a powerful Dreamspace where our intuition and universal creative and balancing powers are at play.

Sound

For this Power Tool you will either need a drum, a rattle, mantra or chant (repetitive song) to help you enter a trance state. You can use a recording (also see *Useful*

Resources) or drum, rattle, sing for yourself. Important is that you find a steady rhythm that resonates deeply with you.

I find the heart beat of Mother Earth (a steady single-beat rhythm) good to begin with. Some people find it easiest to use a recording by an experienced shaman or trance drummer. Others prefer to find their own trance inducing rhythms. Play around with it and explore what suits *you* best.

1. Find a safe place where you will be undisturbed for quite a while. Make sure there is nothing that could potentially harm you (for example things lying around that you could bump into).

2. Center your Self and call in your Spirit Helpers to be with you, to protect you on your journey and to guide you back safely. State your intention.

3. When you feel ready, begin to drum, rattle or sing... Let your Self be carried by the rhythm... Your body might begin to move, gently swaying to and fro... Allow every movement to flow freely as it comes up, or stay still... You will know what to do.

4. Keep breathing, following the rhythm, focused and relaxed at the same time... Close your eyes or leave them open... Stay with the rhythm...

5. Allow the rhythm to take over. There is nothing but the rhythm... You *are* the rhythm...

   Continue for about 10-15 minutes to start with.

6. You can set yourself a timer or an alarm so that you can fully focus and let go. Once you hear its signal, take a few deep belly breaths, stop drumming and slowly bring your Self back to your everyday reality.

Once you feel more and more comfortable and at ease going through the portal into a trance state and back (!), you can extend the duration.

Movement – dancing, shaking, swaying

There are a lot of traditions that use body movement to induce a trance state. The Persian Dervishes are famous for their wild whirling dances, a part of Sama, a ceremony that involves dance and singing to enter an ecstatic trance state to communicate with god or a universal life-giving source. Watch their wild swirling moves on youtube[5] if you are interested.

There are many other ceremonies and rituals performed by indigenous people all over the world that include whirling, stomping, swaying, shaking your body. As said before: some people enter a trance state involuntarily when dancing amongst others on the dance floor. You might have experienced beginning trance stages at a party.

To make it easy I recommend using "trance inducing music" or a pre-recorded trance inducing rhythm. There are many around online – I have listed a few suggestions at the end of this book (see *Useful Resources*). Test various recordings until you find one that supports you best.

Choose a form of movement and keep at it – don't change the movement during the practise. You can experiment with various forms of movement, of course, but don't mix them all up in one practise session " ☺

Examples of movements:

Swaying – rock your upper body back and forth in a steady rhythm (in sync with the music). You can combine the movement with your breath to enhance the effect: breathe in when moving back, breathe out when moving forward.

Shaking – stand upright, with you knees slightly bend, and start shaking your body by bending your knees up and down. Let all your limbs and other body parts go limp, like a puppet, and allow the movement to flow freely through your whole body. Allow your head to shake wildly and your arms to flap around you.

Keep your breath in sync with your movements.

I suggest that you keep your feet on the ground in the beginning and only shake your body by bending your knees. When you have used this Tool a couple of times and feel more at ease, you might want to start stomping and dancing around while you are shaking. Follow your intuition with this.

Swirling – rotating movements have a huge impact on us. They literally propel us out of our thinking mind into a different state of being. This is why a lot of people love merry-go-rounds and why you can see little children spin around until they fall, laughing and shouting with joy. Old spiritual and shamanic traditions have studied the effects of swirling since ancient times and use it as a powerful Tool to enter trance state.

Make sure that there is nothing around that you could hurt you. Align your movements with the music/rhythm and keep going. Don't be afraid to fall. You most likely will, sooner or later – that is part of the experience ☺

If you feel nauseous, dizzy or have any other unpleasant symptoms, please stop immediately. Our bodies show us when we need to be careful, take things easy, and when to stop doing something. Listen to your body and you will be safe. Entering trance states is not for everyone – so be wise and follow the signs ☺

1. Find a safe place where you will be undisturbed for quite a while. Make sure there is nothing that could potentially harm you (for example: things lying around that you could bump into).

2. Center your Self and call in your Spirit Helpers to be with you, to protect you on your journey and to guide you back safely. State your intention.

3. Start the music and begin to move your body. It is important that your moves are repetitive and in sync with the music/rhythm. They often are staccato-like or in a fast flow.

It helps me to move quite fast. However, I have met people who find it easier to enter trance state when they keep a steady slow flow. Experiment and play around to find out what works best for *you*.

4. Allow about 10-15 minutes for a start to experience your Self with this Tool. As above: you can set a timer or alarm so that you don't have to think about time. Once you feel confident and at ease with this Tool you may want to extend the duration of your practise. Just make sure that you are always able to come back easily.

Other Trance triggers

Take something away

People use and have used all sorts of ways to enter a trance. They have taken away things that are a normal component of everyday life for a certain period of time to catapult themselves into an extraordinary state of being. Taking away eating, for example, which is commonly called fasting, is widely known as a method to enter trance states. The deprivation of food, sleep, the company of other people (= being alone), light (= being in complete darkness), gravity (= being in a floatation tank with water) can work wonders and open the doors to trance.

Add something

Another method is to add a component into your life that triggers an altered state of mind: apart from music/rhythms and movement as shown above fragrances or psychoactive substances (= substances that change your perception and effect how you feel and see reality) can be used to enter trance states. Please be aware: The Spirits of psychoactive plants are VERY powerful and definitely not recommended for any experiments! Shamans and healers of all times have to gather a lot of experience and wisdom before they are able to navigate these powerful energies. Please don't try to "do this at home" as it most likely will severely harm you and others. Fragrances (for example incense sticks, smudging, aroma therapy), on the other hand, are generally safe to use.

Toolbox 2 – self-induced trance

Self-induced trance means that you enter a trance state without any external support: no music and no wild dancing – you use your mind and imagination to get you there. The following Tools are great to train your visualisation and concentration muscles. They are also useful when you are in a situation where you cannot move (for example when you are sick and bed-bound) or make some noise.

Self-suggestion, Self-Hypnosis

Before you go to sleep and enter Dreamworld your body normally feels heavy and warm. Heaviness and warmth seem to be two factors that help us to go through the portal and enter trance state. In fact, heaviness is simply a sign that our muscles are completely relaxed – which then leads to an even deeper relaxation, in particular of our vascular system = our blood vessels: the blood flows more freely and we feel warm.

You can induce this state voluntarily by using visualisation. Paint an image of "heaviness" and "warmth" in your head engaging all your senses. Imagine yourself going all floppy and relaxed... *Feel* it in your body... Imagine your shoulders becoming very heavy and completely relaxed... *Feel* it... Imagine the sun warming your skin... and actually *feel* the warmth of the sunrays.

1. As usual: find a quiet space where you feel safe and comfortable. Some find it easier to "dream" when the light is not too bright and the place is warm.

2. When you first start using this exercise you may want to lie down to be able to completely let go and relax. Find a comfortable position, you might want to use a pillow or a blanket to support your body.

3. Take a few deep belly breaths and close your eyes. Closing your eyes will help you to focus at first. As you become more adept you can experiment with open eyes and in busier places – until, eventually, you will be able to enter a completely relaxed state within seconds simply by calling up the memory of this exercise.

4. Take a walk through your body:

    Start with your feet. See them in your mind... *Feel* all the tiny bones in your feet... Relax the muscles and tissue that hold them together... *Feel* the release...

Now, slowly, in your own time, move up your legs... *Feel* your legs heavily on the ground... totally relaxed and heavy... let go...

Move up... along your thighs... to your buttocks... Tense and release them...

Breathe deeply, and with each out-breath sink deeper into relaxing your muscles...

Move up your spine... Relax... Allow yourself to be carried...

Relax your shoulders... your neck... your head...

Move to the front of your body... to the place between your eyebrows... *Feel* the pulsating energy there... Move down to your eyes... Relax them in their sockets...

Go on to your throat... Relax all the muscles there, *feel* how they loosen up...

Continue to your chest, your heart... Relax... Let go...

... down to your belly... breathe deeply into your belly... *Feel* how heavy you are... carried... relaxed...

Feel the warmth that flows through your whole body...

5. When you are ready, slowly come back to your everyday reality, stretch your body and open your eyes to be fully present again with what goes on around you.

If you practise this regularly, you will soon reach a stage where you can enter a state of deep relaxation simply by remembering this Tool and by saying or thinking: "My whole body is heavy, warm and deeply relaxed."

This state of deep relaxation is the platform on which you can build further exercises. It is key to entering the world of Magic and Dreams, and it will also help you to use the other Tools in this book more efficiently. Use it often, to calm down and to center your Self.

Tips:

1. If you find it challenging to feel your body relax, tense the muscles in a particular body part and then deliberately release the tension. Only do this a few times when you start using this Tool in order to get a feeling for the release. Otherwise you might install a habit in your body to tense up before relaxing.

2. Some people find it helpful to speak words while they are going through their body: "My right foot is heavy... really heavy..." Try it and see if it works for you, too.

Be your own alarm clock

Here is another fun Tool that can bring you to the next level of the "Trance game": play with your ability to "set time". Before you go to sleep, think of a time when you want to wake up – without your alarm clock or your mum! Visualise the exact time in your head – and trust that you will wake up.

I sometimes play a variation of this game and ask ask to be woken up at the "right time", for example when I want to perform a dawn ritual or use the early morning hours to write. I fully trust that I will wake up at the exact time that I need to – and it always works for me.

By using this Tool you will hone your skills to manage your own reality and eventually be able to access a trance state voluntarily. It will also assist you to actively shape your life: for example, to attract a certain outcome in your relationship with a friend, your next basketball game or any other situation in your life. Over time you will be able to actively co-create more and more of your experiences. This doesn't mean that you don't have to train for the next football game or to learn for your exam anymore. It means that you will be able to bring your body and mind in the best possible position to attract the best possible outcome – without letting negative energies (worries, fear, doubt, anger, frustration, etc.) affect and distract you.

As said before: using this Tool in a way that might harm or negatively affect others will always backfire in the long run. We are not separate individuals, independent from each other: all life forms are connected with each other like in a huge pulsating net of energy. What you do at any one place in this net will be felt anywhere else.

When you are able to deliberately evoke a deeply relaxed and warm feeling in your body and when you can control your own "time mechanism", you are ready to walk through the portal and enter a deeper trance state at will.

1. Find a quiet and comfortable place where you won't be distracted. Put on your safety belt (= let somebody know what you are doing).

2. Bring up the feeling of deep relaxation and warmth... Breathe deeply and slowly...

   Imagine a portal in front of you. Call your Spirit Helpers and wait until you can feel them... Ask them to watch over you and to bring you back to the portal when you need to return.

3. Watch how the portal opens slowly... Observe the scene... If you see anything that makes you feel uncomfortable or hesitant, STOP. If everything feels fine, walk through the portal... Breathe deeply... and observe what happens...

4. If you come with a question or a request, express it now... Send it out in thought form or mind pictures... See how the words or thoughts or images are "swept away" by a light breeze... and then keep breathing... and see what happens next...

5. You will feel when it is time to "go back" and return to your everyday reality.

The Art of Dreaming

age 12+

The Zen teacher Chuang Tzu dreamed he was a butterfly. When he woke, he wondered, "Am I a man who dreamt about being a butterfly? Or am I really a butterfly who now dreams about being a man?"

Have you ever woken up from a dream and wished you could have changed the ending? Or done something completely differently? Do you wish you could consciously beam yourself into other worlds and realities, do things you can't do easily in your physical reality, like flying, for example? Do you want to consciously access Dreamworld to gain guidance and answers on burning questions in your life?

This Power Tool is a first basic tool that will prepare you and show you a way to learn how to do this. It takes practice and persistence to get visible results – be patient and have fun with it and enjoy experimenting. Before we start the practise part I will give you a brief overview on the "Art of Dreaming".

What are dreams? We all dream at night, even if we sometimes don't remember our dreams. And even if we do, we might just remember the bit where we were chased by a 3-legged rabbit or some other strange detail – and dismiss it as nonsense. Our ancestors, however, have taken dreams very seriously and worked with them since ancient times. Seers and many religious leaders received prophetic messages in their dreams. The indigenous people of Australia traditionally navigate through their physical life by connecting deeply to the Dreamworld. Tibetan Buddhists developed the art of "Dream Yoga", and in our modern society scientists research and acknowledge the "hidden" realms of dreams and their influence on our lives.

A lot of famous inventors, politicians, war chiefs, writers and other individuals received important messages and insights in their dreams and consciously accessed Dreamworld to find guidance and answers to many questions. Dreams can be seen as a portal to an unseen realm where divine, supernatural, immaterial powers communicate with us.

There are different kinds of dreams. Some dreams reflect our "state of mind": If you are stressed, if you had painful or unpleasant experiences during the day, if you are worried about things or sad, this can "play out" in your dreams. Dreams also often help us to process issues and challenges we are dealing with in our everyday waking life.

Dreams can bring up things that we aren't aware of: hopes, fears, experiences of the past, solutions that go beyond our "conscious mind". Those kind of dreams usually depend on your interpretation: when you wake up and remember (parts of) your dream, you review the dream images through your personal "lens" and give them a personal meaning – or not.

There are also other dreams that come from a deeper place leading you further into the realms of Dreamworld. They go way beyond your own personal reality. As you work with this Power Tool you will have more and more dreams that you can a) remember vividly and b) actively participate in. These dreams are sometimes called vivid or clear dreams. Over time you might reach a state where you are able to consciously participate and navigate in Dreamworld quite the same as you would in your awake-state. Master dreamers and so-called lucid dreamers enter and navigate Dreamworld consciously and connect with levels and aspect of themselves and of Life in general that give them a clearer understanding of what's going on in life. It took me over 10 years of practise to first experience such a dream level consciously – having said this: I believe that it is totally possible to reach this state much faster, sometimes instantly ☺

Again and again: take it easy and play with it. The more relaxed and playful you are, the easier for you to open your channels and find pathways into the Dreamworld.

1. Sensitization – raising your awareness

If you want to consciously travel into the World of Dreams and be aware of what's happening there, you can start practising a few useful skills while you are awake:

mindfulness practises like *Journey into your heart, Finding your rhythm, Breathing with River,* meditation or simply paying attention to what's going on around you while you are awake; for example noticing the "small things" like the sun on your skin, the birdsong, the shape of a particular cloud...

As you become more and more aware about these little details, your dreams will become more vivid and you will remember them more clearly. You will also notice more and more differences between the feeling of dream reality and awake-reality. This is a first step to become aware in a dream that you are actually dreaming (which is sometimes called "lucid dreaming").

Once you are able to discern between dream and awake-reality, you might want to try the following to consciously enter Dreamworld: set an alarm for 3am. This is a special time when it is easiest for most of us to go through the portal and to enter Dreamworld consciously. It has to do with human sleep patterns and the influence of the position of the sun and the stars at that time of day or rather: night. If you are like me and truly dislike alarm clocks, set your intention to wake up at 3am and ask your Spirit Helpers to make sure that you will wake up "in time". It always works for me – if I really mean it and if it is meant to be. Try it.

When you wake up, keep the light dimmed and stay in a sleepy, dreamily state as much as possible without completely nodding off into deep sleep again. The art is to stay in between awake and deep sleep mode. It helps me to focus on the darkness on the back of my eyelids and to lie really still. I set a clear intention that I want to enter Dreamworld and to stay fully conscious and in control of what is happening.

Sometimes I get up, wrap myself into a warm blanket and meditate. The meditation helps me to enter Dreamworld consciously, and the sitting position helps me to avoid drifting back to deep unconscious sleep. Find out what works for *you*!

Observe the dream images that show up, and try to stay aware that you are dreaming. This takes a little practise, but is really fun after a while when you manage to do it.

2. Writing the story of your dream

Once you have mastered the first step and feel you can enter Dreamworld consciously and at will while staying aware of what is happening, you might want to move on to the next level. On this level you will influence what is happening in your dream.

Practise when you normally go to bed, or keep your "3am routine", if this works better for you. 3am works well for me, as I am often either too tired or too much "in my mind" at night before I go to bed.

Observe the images that show up once you entered Dreamworld. Try to change or influence little things. Let's say you are in a house together with many people. Try to walk towards someone and speak to that person. Or try to explore the house and move freely through the rooms.

Once you can do this, experiment with other things. Things you cannot normally do when you are in awake-mode. I love to go through walls, for example. Flying is also exciting! Maybe you had "flying dreams" before, but without *consciously choosing* to fly. It is really fun to practise flying at will when you are in Dreamworld. I find it quite useful, too, to escape all sorts of not-so-nice situations... Flying can be hard work or it can be completely effortless and easy. Some people find it frightening, others love it.

Observe yourself and go with what feels good for you. You can "push your boundaries" in Dreamworld, but keep in mind: all these Tools are here to serve you and others. You can challenge your Self, however, make sure that you always feel ok with what is happening. If you feel uncomfortable, if you feel you cannot handle things in a good way, remember that you can always STOP and wake up. This is very important to know: **You can choose to end the experience and to wake up at any point in your dream journey!** Taking control is necessary to keep you safe – not only in Dreamworld, but always in your life.

General advice: Please be patient. Some people have no trouble at all with entering Dreamworld and practising lucid dreaming. Others, like me, take a long time before they can consciously navigate through their dreams. What

I am trying to say: Enjoy the journey and keep playing – the rewards of mastering the Art of Dreaming are manifold and well worth it.

In indigenous traditions, shamans and healers often use special rituals and ceremonies involving rattles and drums to enter Dreamworld (also see *Trance –Portal to the Otherworld*). Sometimes, they take herbal substances to enhance their "dream vision". Please don't try this at home. There is a lot of knowledge, self-awareness and experience necessary to safely do this. I know of many cases where the experiment with substances went wrong: sleep paralysis, paranoia, hallucinations, nightmares are only some of the not-so-nice things that can happen as a consequence. Be aware: herbal (or other) substances often hold or trigger powerful energies – from my experience you need a certain expertise and consciousness to handle them safely. Otherwise their powerful energies will distract you from your Self and completely overwhelm you. And: as a Power Kid you most likely won't need additional assistance anyway! Most kids I have met who are born after 1992 already come with very refined "connection channels" and Super Powers and have the capacity to use these Power Tools without the need for external triggers.

Once you can roam Dreamworld while being fully aware that you are dreaming, and once you can control the story of your dream, you have mastered the first level of the Art of Dreaming! Congratulation!

Tips:

1. Sometimes, especially when you are more advanced with this Tool, your dream-reality can become so real that you might get confused and be unsure if you are dreaming or not. Please be aware of your safety: you don't want to jump from the top of a skyscraper in your awake-consciousness, whereas you can quite safely do this in Dreamworld. So before doing anything "bold" or potentially dangerous, I quickly do a simple check: I poke my hand through a solid object (a tree, wall, furniture, stone or whatever I can find around me). If I can do this without hurting myself, then I "know" I am in Dreamworld. If not... then I better don't jump off that ledge ☺

2. Call in your Spirit Helpers before you enter Dreamworld and ask them to "keep an eye on you". Mine helped me out more than once when I encountered tricky situations or didn't know what to do.

3. When you feel ready and quite adept with these Power Tools, you might want to explore more options and advanced levels of the Art of Dreaming (for example Lucid Dreaming and Dream Yoga). You will find inspiration online and through your Spirit Helpers.

MAGIC LIFE ART

Magic Life Art

Creating art is creating Magic. Your whole life is an art project: every experience, every choice you make is an expression of your Self, is your Life Art. Make it an act of power (also see *Your Act of Power*) and consciously create your Life Art. You choose the colours and materials you want to use. You choose the shapes and forms. You choose how simple or how complex your artwork will be. You are the Artist, the Magician and the Creator of your Life. Trust your knowing. Experiment and let your Self free. Let your brain rest. Follow your heart and do what is fun.

No matter if you consider yourself an "arty person" or not: all of us are Life Artists. The activities and ideas on the following pages support you to bring out your inner Creator, your inner Artist, your inner Life Designer. Art is playful creation – and a fun and simple way to discover your own Magic powers.

If you don't feel like reading through the text, then you most likely won't need any of my suggestions ☺ Just dismiss them and find your own ways of creative expression!

Art is Magic and the water of Life. Water is free. So drink, and be filled up.

Let's play and create some Magic!

Earth Mandalas

all ages

You might have heard the word "mandala" before. Mandala is a Sanskrit word and means "circle". In Hindu and Buddhism it represents the Universe. Mandala colouring books are popular to help us focus on the circular matrix that is the basis of all Life. Colouring in mandalas or creating your own mandala drawings has a calming and centering effect on many people. Try it and find out if it works for you, too.

In this chapter I want to share another form of creating mandalas. Have you ever heard of crop circles[6]?

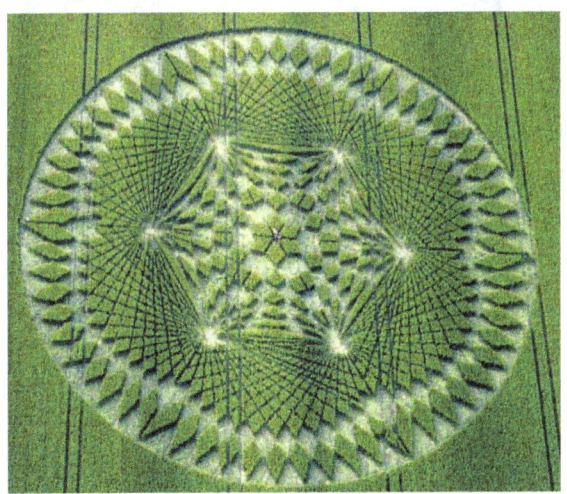

No matter who created them (there are various theories, from extraterrestrials to human artists to farmers who just want to have a bit of fun and attract tourists to their place): These giant mandalas hold high energy that can be felt and measured. Like Stonehenge and other ancient Power Places in Nature they concentrate energy, and if you go there you will be able to increase your energy levels = your energy will be uplifted.

There are other places that have the adverse effect: they drain your energy levels and exhaust you. The more you work with this book and develop your skills with the Power Tools, the more you will be able to detect differences in energy within and around you. You will be able to discern exactly between what gives you energy and what drains your energy levels.

Creating mandalas on the Earth uplifts the energy of a certain place. Crop circles definitely do this – if you get a chance to visit a crop circle you will feel it. I encourage you to create your own Earth Mandalas to honour Earth energy and to increase the energy of a place. Your Earth Mandalas are a gift to the Earth and can help balance some of the destructive effects human activity has on this Planet.

1. Choose a place. You can do it wherever you go, during a walk through the forest or the nearby park, at the beach, in your garden... wherever you feel drawn to.
2. Set your intention. Do you want to uplift this particular place because there is a lot of pollution? Do you simply want to acknowledge the place and honour Mother Earth energy?
3. Briefly sit or lie down and connect. Breathe deeply and feel yourself commingle with the place.
4. If you want, call in your Spirit Helpers and ask for their assistance. They are with you all the time, and the more you work with them, the more intimate and instant your connection will be. Calling them in makes it easier for them to actively support you.
5. When you are ready, wander around aimlessly and gather what attracts your attention in front of your feet and eyes: stones, twigs, feathers, leaves, cones, shells...
6. Once you feel that you have "enough for now", bring it to the spot where you want to create your mandala. There will be an "energy center" - you will know where it is: place the first stone or object there as an anchor. This doesn't need to be the center of your mandala. Then continue to place all the other things.

I personally like to simply start, placing my gathered objects intuitively following my "gut feeling". Others like to create a design in their heart and mind before they start, for example by marking a circle with a stick and a piece of string and placing a stone or other special object in the center. Do what you feel drawn to!

7. When you have finished your mandala, you might feel how the energy shifts. Maybe it already shifted while you were building the mandala.

8. Before you leave the place, please don't forget to cleanse your Self. This is especially important if you chose a place that needed balancing. Like said before: We are exposed to various energies every day, and in the same way as we are "gathering dust" during the day and need a shower at night, we also need to clean our energy field. You can do this in a simple way by placing your palms flat on the ground and imagine how any energy that you don't need flows out through your hands and dissipates into the soil. If you feel that there were strong energies at play, you might want to do a cleansing ritual at a river, lake, ocean or other natural water source. If this isn't possible or easy, then simply have a shower at home: let water run over your whole body, including your head, until you feel totally clear and free (also see *Cleansing and clearing*).

Make your own Trance instrument

> all ages

Younger ones might need assistance for some of the steps or can choose an easy version.

Rattles are amazing tools. You find them everywhere: babies have them, musicians all over the world use them, rattle snakes rattle their tail to scare intruders away, and carnival goers in Europe still use rattles as a remnant of old rituals to scare the harsh Winter "Demons" away.

What is it that makes rattles special and omnipresent? Researchers found that rattles harmonise and increase our brain activity. They help us to merge the conscious and the unconscious and to enter a state of trance (deep relaxation and expanded awareness, also see *Trance – Portal to the Otherworld*). Humans used them since ancient times to walk through the portal into other realities, to perform healing rituals, to cleanse and protect spaces – and to relax babies ☺

Rattles are easy to make – and like with everything you create: it is fun and powerful to make your own. You don't need to buy expensive materials. You can find them everywhere: at the beach, in the forest, at the river, in a park, garden, natural reserve. You can also use recycled materials such as empty yoghurt containers or plastic pipes to build a rattle. I personally prefer natural materials because of the energy they carry. By using natural materials you also reduce plastic waste. A hollow bamboo cane filled with rice, beans, small pebbles, crystal splinters or other contents (see below) and sealed off at both ends makes a perfect magic Tool that you can use in many ways.

Here are a few examples to inspire you – there are many more "out there" and the possibilities are infinite. Your imagination is the limit.

Gourd rattles

Pumpkins, squash and gourds are all part of the *Cucurbitaceae* family. They have been and are still providing food for humans and other animals, and when dried they can also be used as vessels and instruments. They transform automatically into natural rattles if you leave them at their vines: after a couple of months (depending on the weather conditions) they dry out, and the dried seeds provide a natural filling producing a rattling sound.

There are literally hundreds of videos on youtube to show you how to grow and prepare gourds or pumpkins to make a rattle if you need more inspiration. Here a few easy steps to make your own magic gourd rattle:

1. Get a pumpkin (gourd, squash) from your garden, the farmer's market or the supermarket. You can grow your own in a bucket or planter box, too – just make sure that you have a LOT of space around the bucket as the plant will spread out.

Choose a small-sized pumpkin variety. Bottle shapes are nice, but you can also use round ones or UFO-shaped ones.

2. Let the pumpkin dry: either on the vine (if you grow your own) or outside, preferably on a rack in a dry and airy space. The skin will go all mouldy and yucky – so make sure there are no animals around. If you have a shed or garage or other indoor space that is not inhabited by humans or animals, hang up the pumpkin in an old onion bag, for example, and it will dry faster. The more sun and the dryer the weather the faster it dries. It can take up to a couple of months, though. Usually I let my pumpkins dry over winter, and they are ready by spring to be worked on.

The pumpkin is ready when it feels light, its skin is peeling off and its outside is hard like a shell. When you shake it, you most likely will hear a few dried seeds rattling inside.

3. Clean your pumpkin. You need to clean off the mould and the black or grey old skin. I recommend using gloves to avoid direct contact with the mould. Gently rub off the skin with a scouring pad or brush. If it doesn't come off easily you might want to soak the pumpkin for a couple of hours in warm water – don't worry, it won't soften.

Once the skin is clean and nice (there might be a few marks from the mould, but they make up the special character and beauty of your pumpkin), let it dry on a rack in an airy space until it is completely dry.

You can either use the rattle as it is, if there are enough seeds inside to make a nice sound. Or, in most cases, you might want to add more "stuff" to create a better rattling sound. You can use whatever materials you have access to, preferably natural materials to keep the energies pure: seeds and seedpods, rice, beans, corn, pebbles, crystals, sand, bones... If you want to create your own personal "flavour", you can add things that have a special meaning to you. I filled baby teeth into one of my "transformation" rattles to symbolise the transition from one phase into another.

Step 4 will show you how to add rattling material to your pumpkin.

4. Fill the pumpkin. In order to be able to add things into your pumpkin, you obviously need to open it.

Before you cut the pumpkin open, decide if you want a handle or rather create a shaker-type of rattle. If you choose the first option, find a solid stick that you can use as a handle. It will close the hole in your pumpkin, once you have filled it. You can carve the stick if you want. Make sure it is strong wood that won't break.

Use a carpet knife or other sharp tool to cut out a hole approximately the size of the stick. Younger ones might want to get some support for this step. Be careful – it is easy to break the skin of a dried pumpkin. To avoid cracks you can first punch a circle of little holes with a pricker into the pumpkin, and then carefully cut out the hole with the knife.

Once you have cut out a hole, clean out the inside of the pumpkin to get rid of any mould and other bits you don't need. Protect your nose and mouth with a bandana or something else to not inhale mouldy dust. You can use a piece of bent wire, chop sticks, a spoon, a melon baller or whatever else is suitable for the job to scrape out the pumpkin. Depending on the shape of your pumpkin = if it is not easy to access all parts through the hole, you can use coarse gravel or stones: fill in the gravel and shake the pumpkin. The stones will scrape stuff off and clean the inside.

5. Now that your pumpkin is clean on the inside as well as on the outside, fill in your magic sound beans or

whatever you want to use. Experiment and play around with your fillings until you have the sound you want. As said before: you can use special materials to increase the magic potency of your rattle.

6. All that is left to do now is closing the hole. You might have to fiddle around a bit until the stick or cork fits into the hole perfectly. Use fine sanding paper to carefully make the hole bigger if needed. If it is too big, you might need to wrap fabric or leather around your stick to make it a tight fit.

The stick has to go in quite a bit – otherwise it will "wobble around" when you shake your rattle later on. Some people have the stick go all the way through and come out at the other end – in this case you need to cut two holes. I have also seen rattles with a woven string or leather tape tied around the pumpkin and wrapped tightly around the stick handle to hold it in place. Be creative and find your own way(s) that work best for you.

Once you have adjusted the stick securely in the hole, add glue around the edges to seal it off.

Another option is to simply close the hole with a cork or to glue a piece of leather or strong fabric onto the hole and seal it with sealant or another thick layer of glue around the rim. If you choose this version, you won't have a handle for your rattle. Depending on the shape of your pumpkin, you might want to weave some sort of net around it. That makes it easier to hold and shake your rattle.

7. Decorate your rattle. If you want, you can paint the outside of your pumpkin, attach strings of colourful wool or leather to the handle, add feathers, beads... let your imagination run free!

Clay rattles

Clay is another ancient material that has been and is still used by humans. It is free, it is widely available in the soil, it is very versatile = you can use it in many ways to make all sorts of vessels – and rattles ☺

Clay rattles can take many forms and shapes, from very simplistic to highly elaborate. Here is a simple version to start with:

1. You obviously need clay. If you don't have clayey soil in your front yard or nearby, you can get it from a pottery or a shop for arts and crafts supplies. There are also sources online where you can order potters clay. You can use air dry or kiln dry clay. For the rattle described here you only need a small amount (approximately the size of a tennis ball). You also need a tiny piece of cloth or tissue and a "modelling tool": a thin straight stick is ideal for this; you can also use a chop stick or pencil.

2. Tear off a small piece of clay and form it into 4 to 5 tiny clay balls or beads. These will be your "sound makers". Roll the rest of the clay into a ball.

3. Cut the ball in half with the thin stick.

4. Roll the halves into two balls about the size of a golf ball. Pinch a hole into each ball with your thumb and form two little "pots".

5. Wrap the little bead-balls into a piece of cloth so that they don't stick together, and then put them into one of the "pots".

6. Carefully score the rim of the pots with the stick, add a bit of water and maybe some slip (watery clay that acts as glue) with a paintbrush and stick the two pots together.

7. Use the stick or your hands to smooth the joint until you cannot notice it anymore and the two parts are firmly connected. Roll the rattle back and forth onto a smooth surface to finish it off, and – if needed – even out the surface with a wet paintbrush.

8. Poke small holes into one of the sides of the rattle. This will release air when firing the rattle in the kiln (you don't want it to explode) and also make it sound louder. If you wish, decorate your rattle before you put it into the kiln. You can use the stick to draw patterns into the soft clay. Or use the cap of a bottle or a pen, shells, stamps, etc. to stamp ornaments onto your rattle.

   If you want to paint your rattle, there are many different options. Depending on what paint and procedure you choose, you need to do it before or after drying. As a lot of paints contain chemicals, I don't like to use them. If you want, you can add food colouring or natural colorants like beet root juice to your clay or paint the wet clay before drying (the colours will change through the drying process though).

9. Dry your rattle – either in an airy place or in a kiln, depending what clay you used.

Other rattles

Option 1

1. You need a thin cane, willow or other bendy branch; some natural string, twine or leather tape, dried seedpods, shells or any other natural materials that make a rattling sound; a sharp knife, pricker or pointy tool.

2. Pierce a hole into the seedpods, shells or other materials. Be careful as the delicate objects break easily. The hole needs to be big enough to put the bendy cane through it.

3. Thread the seedpods (or shells) onto the cane. If this is too difficult (for example because the seedpods aren't strong enough and break apart), you can thread them onto string or twine and twist the string tightly around the cane.

4. Bend the cane with the pods into a semi-circle and tie it in place with string, twine or leather tape – et voilà!

5. Decorate your rattle with feathers, beads, etc. if you want to.

Option 2

1. You need a piece of leather, felt or strong fabric, long enough to fit around your ankle, wrist or belly. You can also crochet or weave a band. You also need natural sewing thread; a strong leather needle; rattle fillings (seedpods and shells are great for this kind of rattle).

2. Make or cut a band that fits around your ankle or wrist out of your preferred material. You can also make a rattle belt that goes around your waist. You will then need a longer band.
3. Punch little holes into the seedpods, shells or other rattle fillings. You can use a sharp pointy knife, puncher, hot needle, pricker, a very fine drill or whatever else seems suitable. Be careful as dried seedpods or shells tend to break easily.
4. Attach the seedpods/shells to the band using the natural sewing thread.
5. Decorate your rattle if you want.

This kind of rattle is great when you dance or move around and want your hands free.

Various ways of using your rattle

Before I describe some ways that I (and others) have explored, I want to tell you: there is often no right or wrong way in Magic. Important is that you trust your Self! Trust your knowing. You will feel which hand to use and how to shake your rattle. With this in mind, here a few methods that have worked for me/others that you might want to experiment with:

1. To enter a trance

Steady rhythm next to your ear/head – shake rattle back and forth, "hammering"

Hold the rattle close to your head, next to your ear, and rattle in a steady fast rhythm. Find out what works for you – I like it pretty fast. It helps me "switch the planes" rather quickly.

Keep going. Even if the rattling noise is unnerving. After a while you will enter a "different state" of mind... Allow that to happen... Just keep rattling. You will know when to stop.

2. To attract energy into the body & to collect energy

Spiralling, moving towards the body

I usually use my left hand and shake the rattle lightly in a downward spiralling movement directing it to the point where I want the energy to enter the body.

This method can be helpful when you feel weak or sad or otherwise not in balance to bring supportive and uplifting energies into your body. You can heal bruises, stomachache or headache, and uplift your Self when you feel down, angry, upset.

You can collect supportive energy, for example from the stars, and direct it wherever you need it with your rattle.

Some people recommend an anticlockwise spin for attracting energies. Experiment with different directions and trust your knowing and intuition. Follow what feels "right" for you.

3. To extract energy out of the body

Spiralling, moving away from the body

I use my right hand, shaking the rattle in an upward spiralling movement (clockwise, most of the time ;). Often, it is a faster movement than when I want to attract energy. Let the rhythm and movement come to you.

You can use this method to get rid of energies that affect you (or others) in a negative way. Imagine that you are sucking the negative energy out with the sound of your rattle. Be aware where you direct the unwanted energy. I usually direct it deep into the Earth. To do this I shake the rattle with a sharp movement towards the ground, as if shaking out a wet paintbrush. I do this a couple of times, until I feel the energy is "gone".

4. *To give energy back*

Up and down shake, staccato, snakelike movement

When you want to balance an energy field (of a place or a person), harmonise energy or give back energy that you don't need or want, shake your rattle in a short staccato movement.

Either just disperse the energy around you or direct it where you want it with your rattle.

5. *"Rattlesnake Rattle" – "I am here"*

Fast shaking (small movements), like a rattlesnake rattle, breaks in between "rattles"

You can use this rolling rattling for various purposes (see below). Like the rattle of a rattlesnake it tells your surroundings that you are here.

To greet a place/space

Use the Rattlesnake Rattle when you come to a place where you want to perform a ritual or do your practice or whenever you visit a new place in order to greet the Spirits of the Land and all the other beings.

To rebalance

When you feel out of balance, the Rattlesnake Rattle is a good way to bring you back to your Self, to calm and soothe your Self. It can help you to refocus and to reconnect with your Self.

To divert confusion

The Rattlesnake Rattle is also a great way to become fully present in the here and now. Rattle and listen to the rolling sound until you feel centered and calm.

6. *To accompany a song and create rhythm*

Shake your rattle back and forth in a semi-circle

A rattle is, of course, also a musical instrument. It is easy to transport and a great rhythm instrument for many occasions. You can accompany yourself singing a song and play together with others. You can play steady rhythms to induce calm and altered states of mind. Or you can go absolutely wild and crazy to release whatever it is you need to release. Happy rattling!

Altar – creating a sacred space

all ages

Do you know what an altar is?

The name "altar" originally comes from the Latin word "altus" meaning "high". It was and is used in the Christian tradition to describe a place where sacred objects and offerings to "Higher Spirits" like gods and deities are placed and rituals are performed. In many cultures around the world people have altars in their houses or outside to mark the space where they pray or communicate with their ancestors and Spirit Beings. If you are a part of a religious tradition such as Christianity or Buddhism, you will be familiar with altars. The Islam is one of the few religions I know of that doesn't have altars, because its followers say that you can pray everywhere and don't need a special place to do that.

As a child I loved to create a special table with stones, feathers, crystals and other objects that were meaningful to me. I also had a little brass bowl with holy water that I regularly got from churches in our neighbourhood. Even though my family isn't Christian and I wasn't raised in this tradition, I liked going to old churches in the area where I grew up. I loved the serenity and stillness there and the beautiful stained glass windows. A lot of old churches in Europe are build on Power Places with special energies. This can help you enter into other realities, reflect and feel deeply on Life matters, and pray or communicate with Spirit World.

The Christian custom to sprinkle holy water over something or someone to cleanse and connect the object or the person to the Spirit World somehow made sense to me. So I made sure I always had my wee bowl filled with holy water. I would rub a few drops of water on my "third eye" (the place between the eyebrows), long before I learned the name of this body part and its meaning. It made me feel cleansed, protected and ready to pray. It would calm me down. "Praying" to me simply meant that I would get in touch with a higher force. I didn't call it god and hadn't really a name for it. It was just a sense of a powerful force that I knew was beyond me and my body and that would steer and manage all Life. I would have long chats with this "force", share all my worries, fears, frustrations, ask for advice, help, support – and usually feel really thankful, settled and calm at the end of my "prayers".

I also liked candles on my altar. I made my own out of wax that I collected from old burnt-down candles and beeswax sheets that I got from my brother who was a beekeeper (see *Playing with Fire* if you want to make your own beeswax candle). Somehow, my altar was a special go-to place for me: in calm periods of my life I lit a candle, said brief words of thanks, and that was it. It was whenever the going got tough that I spent more time. It helped me a lot to sit there and vent things. To share my worries and sorrows. To cry and to ask for advice and guidance. I would hold one of my crystals or special stones and ask for assistance. I would send my burning questions and requests up into the sky with the smoke of some incense. The warm yellow light, the sweet beeswax smell and the magic of the steady flame of a candle calmed down my racing mind and emotions. And always, always I would feel better, more centered and relieved at the end.

Later in my life, when I started to move around and change houses and locations more often, I became more and more independent from my altar. From a permanent place in my home it shifted to outdoor places: Power Places in Nature, a place next to a river, a tree, a rock became my altars.

Nowadays, I still have my sacred objects around me at a special place in my home. I don't really need them to pray: I pray wherever I go and wherever I am. I find special places and natural altars everywhere. Nevertheless, I love connecting and playing with my Sacred Helpers at home. They carry special energies that support me, and they are reminders in my home to help me stay focused.

If you feel like creating your own altar, here a few ideas to inspire you:

1. Setting an intention

Why do you want to create an altar? What do you want it for?

Set a clear intention. For example, you might want to create a place where you can talk to your Spirit Helpers or Guardian Angels on a regular basis. Or you need healing and want to create a special healing altar. Or you might simply want to create a special place to connect to your Self, to focus and pray/communicate with Spirit.

You can create many different altars for different purposes. Or you can have one altar as a special go-to-place and rearrange it for different occasions.

2. Calling in Elemental Energies

In many traditions and cultures people use the Elements or symbols representing the Elemental Forces on their altar. I have already talked about the four main elements in the chapter *Rituals & ceremonies*. Having some representatives of the Elemental Forces around will help you to call in their energies and to center your Self. All Elemental Forces support you in finding balance and inspiration in their own ways.

Candles represent **Fire** energies: creativity, inspiration, will power and strength.

To call in **Water** energies, you can use fresh pure water in a little bowl or cup: water from a natural source like a river, lake, ocean, rain is ideal, but tap water will do, too, if you don't have that. You can also use representatives such as shells, corals, dried seaweed or an image of a dolphin, fish or another water creature. Use whatever helps you to connect with Water energies: intuition, nurturing, gentleness and balance.

Feathers and/or incense sticks are often used as symbol for **Air** energies: knowledge and power of the mind, flexibility, courage and perseverance.

Carriers of **Earth** energies are stones and crystals, seeds and seedpods, flowers, potted plants, images of turtles, moles or other land animals that remind you of Mother Earth. Earth energies will especially help you to ground your Self and to feel safe, balanced and confident.

3. Connecting with Spirit & universal Life Force

Your altar can be a safe protected space where you enter Spirit World and connect with what I call universal Life Force (= the Life giving and driving force behind all that is). Choose something that represents Spirit or Soul energies for you. I used to have a prism-shaped crystal hanging above my altar as it would reflect rainbow-coloured rays and remind me of the many colours of Life and Soul.

Find your own symbol(s). You will know what to use – trust your intuition.

4. Inviting Ancestors, Spirit Helpers, Angels and other Beings

If it feels right for you, you can invite supportive energies of your ancestors (known or unknown to you) by placing images or other objects that remind you of them onto your altar. The people who walked the land before us are often waiting for us to connect with them. If we invite them into our lives, they are supporting us with their wisdom.

You can also call in helpers from the Spirit World to support you on your journey: Spirit Helpers, Guardian and other Angels, Plant and Animal Spirits (Devas, Totem Animals). Choose objects that anchor their energies onto your altar: images, hair/fur, dried leaves, bark, flowers...

Happy creating ☺

Tips:

1. In this chapter, I only listed a few ideas that you might want to include when creating your altar. You don't need to use any of them. As it is *your* special place, please let your Self run free and use whatever fills your altar with meaning and brings it alive for *you*.

2. Creating your unique altar – a place for prayer, magic and power – can be a very powerful experience. It can be a portal for you to enter Magic and Spirit World. As always: follow what feels good and is fun for you.

Power Pouch

all ages

Let's make a magic bag where you can store special objects: things that remind you of how powerful you are. Things that have a special meaning to you. Things that remind you of your connection to your Spirit Helpers. Things that bring up Magic in you and that you can use to create Magic in your life. Things that remind you of a turning point or special moment in your life.

Create your own Power Pouch as a symbol for balance and power and your connection to other realms of Magic, Dreams and Spirit.

Many indigenous cultures have so-called medicine bags. The bags and their contents tell a lot about who the person is. They are also said to protect their carriers and hold sacred objects that represent and store the vitality and unique power of the carrier. Some people identify so much with their medicine bag that they are devastated when it gets stolen or when they lose it. They feel as if they lose their life force and their power.

When making your own Power Pouch or medicine bag, you can go as fancy and complex as you like. I personally like to keep things simple and practical, so I chose to share this relatively simple method to create your own. You will find many more examples on youtube if you search for "leather drawstring bag" or "leather pouch".

The "specialness" of your Power Pouch comes from the objects that you put into it or rather from the meaning that those objects hold for you. You can create a simple bag without much "fluff & frills" – or you can spend time and love to decorate it with feathers, beads, coloured wool and whatever else you like.

Do what feels right to *you* and enjoy the process.

1. Choose a material for your bag. You can use any fabric or cloth, leather, felt or other materials that seem suitable to you. Make sure they are hard-wearing and strong enough to hold and protect pointy objects (crystals, for example). Preferably use natural materials, as they carry a different energy than processed materials such as plastic fiber and synthetics.

   Furniture shops sometimes give away old leather sample books for free. You can also source suitable materials at recycling stores or charity shops.

   In addition, you will need a marker pen; scissors; some string, waxed twine or scrap pieces of material; a strong leather needle and decoration materials (optional).

   To tie your pouch you can either use shoestring, leather tape, string or cut stripes from scrap pieces that are left over from your bag.

2. Decide how big you want your pouch to be. Mark out a circle on your piece of leather or fabric, depending on the size you want, and cut it out. You can use a

salad bowl, saucer or other round object to get it perfectly round.

If you use soft fabric or cloth, you need to hem it to stop it from frazzling. You can also cut out a second circle, fold the rim of the two circles over (pin it down with needles), then lay the two pieces on top of each other (with the folded sides facing each other), sew along the rim either by hand or with a sewing machine (carefully taking out all the pinning needles while you sew). You will end up with a double-layered nicely lined round shape with a clean hem that won't unravel.

3. Punch or cut holes along the rim with a puncher, pricker or sharp tool. Thread the string, leather tape or whatever else you want to use to tie your bag through the holes (with or without needle, depending on your materials).

If you use soft fabric or cloth: Weave sewing thread with a needle along the rim as a drawstring. You can weave more than one round to make it stronger. At the end, connect the threads with a knot. You could also use eyes through which you thread string or twine if you use thicker materials for your pouch.

4. Decorate your pouch if you feel like it. You can thread beads onto the drawstrings, attach feathers, embroider the pouch with beads, stitchery, shells... Let your imagination run wild!

Reading energy – make your own pendulum

age 8+

Everything is energy.

Some things and beings are dense energy clusters, so we can see them. Others are invisible energy impulses that travel all around and within us.

Our thoughts are energy, our emotions are energy, too. We are sending out and receiving energy all the time. Sensitive people can naturally sense the energies within and around them.

The more you experiment with the Tools in this book the better you will become at reading energy fields and at being aware what energies you are sending out. Being able to do that can help you to navigate through your life with more ease. You will be able to consciously create

Magic in your life and to flow with the current of the energies instead of swimming against it.

In this chapter, I will show you a simple Tool that can assist you to make the energy current within and around you visible. It is like a reading device and can help you until you are able to read energy without it. This Tool has a common name that you might have heard before: it is called a pendulum. The pendulum is moved by energy signals that you are sending out.

Pendulums are and have been also used to discover Earth energy fields ("dowsing"), natural underground sources of water, gold or oil, to locate people, things or animals, for divination and healing, to help people make decisions and for many other purposes.

1. To make your own pendulum, you need a piece of string, wool, an old necklace or whatever else you can find lying around. You also need a bead, a stone, a shell, a key, a ring or something else that will serve you as a weight. Ideally, it already has a hole in it.

2. Attach your weight (bead, stone, shell, ring, etc.) to the string or chain. Adjust the length of the string/chain. Some people recommend 15-20 centimeters. I personally prefer a shorter length. Play around and feel what works best for *you*.

There are many ways to attach your weight to the chain or string. If your weight has a hole, simply thread the string through it. If it doesn't and if it is not easy to make one, you can just wrap the chain or string around the weight or attach it with a piece of wire.

Be creative and add your own ideas.

How to use a pendulum

First: everybody can use a pendulum. Sometimes it takes a while for you to get the hang of it. Keep playing around with it and you will get there.

Here are some guidelines for you to experiment with:

1. Hold the pendulum loosely – this is important so that the energy can flow freely.

   Some hold the pendulum between thumb and index finger, others – like me – let the string or chain run over their index finger.

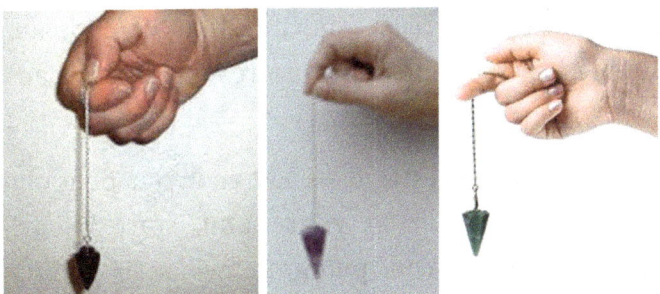

Some hold their hand freely in the air, others place the elbow on a table or other surface to be more stable. Explore what feels natural and easy and what helps you to relax your hand and fingers.

2. Relax, breathe and become calm and still.

You need to be able to get your thoughts and emotions out of the way. As you have probably experienced while working with the Tools in this book, your thoughts and emotions are creating an energy field and thus sending out energy signals. If they are strong in your mind and heart, they can literally "block your sight", and you won't be able to get a clear signal from your pendulum.

In order to get clear results, you need to be as calm and focused as you can be. If you are upset, sad, "fuming", tired, sick, then it is best to use your calm-down & centering Tools *before* you use the pendulum (also see *Code of practice, Letting go I + Letting Go II, The Monkey Mind, Breathing with the River*). Otherwise your thoughts and emotions might influence the movements of the pendulum.

Stay relaxed and trust your intuition. Your pendulum simply makes visible what is already within or around you.

3. When you feel calm and steady and your pendulum is hanging loosely from your hand, start by asking: "What is a YES?" Your pendulum will start moving – it might take a while; just be patient, breathe and observe what is happening. Keep your hand and fingers as still as you can without tensing up.

   Once you know how your pendulum moves to express a "YES", ask: "What is a NO?" Again: it might take a while before the pendulum starts moving. The more relaxed, open and calm you are and the less your thoughts interfere, the faster your pendulum will react. In the beginning, it might only move a little bit. Over time, you will probably notice that the movements become clearer and stronger the more you use it.

   As your pendulum will mainly give you yes/no answers, you will need to ask your questions accordingly. For example, you may ask: "Should I go to the party?" instead of: "Should I go to the party or stay home?"

   If you are looking for underground water or other things, a "YES" movement simply means "it is here", a "NO" movement means "nothing here".

I have been using a pendulum for most of my life and have observed another possible "answer": sometimes, the pendulum doesn't move at all. For me this means: "It doesn't matter what you do." There is no energy pointing in one particular direction. So whatever I decide doesn't really affect my energy much. Using the example above: I can go to the party or stay at home – it doesn't really matter.

If you want, ask: "What is NEUTRAL?" so that you know your pendulum movement for this answer, too.

<u>Please note:</u> Different people get different pendulum movements. For example, my "YES" is a circling movement to the right, my "NO" is a back and forth movement. My "NEUTRAL" is a complete standstill. Your pendulum movements might differ!

Keep playing with your pendulum, and over time you will find your own ways of using this ancient Power Tool to read energy fields.

4. Once you know how your pendulum moves, there are many ways to use it.

You can ask **YES/NO questions** and get answers.

You can also **test, if something is "right" for you**: let's say, for example, you want to find out if a certain remedy has a positive effect on you. Hold the remedy in front of your body. Then bring the pendulum with your other hand between you and the remedy. If it moves back and forth between you and the remedy, the energies are supporting you = you can take the remedy. If the pendulum separates you and the object (= swings from left to right), the energy of the remedy and your energy don't go well together. You can do this little test with any other objects, for example food items, drinks, jewelry (sometimes they carry non-supportive energies) etc.

You can **explore the energy and vitality level** of places, people and objects with a pendulum, too. It will move very strongly (usually in a circular movement), if there is a high-energy field. You can combine this with asking questions such as: "Where are the water lines?", "Where are low energy places in the body that need healing?", "Has this food a lot of vitality (= life energy)?" The stronger the movement, the higher the energy level and vice versa. Water lines create a strong pendulum reaction – try and test your environment for any hidden water lines if you live in a rural area (city areas are usually "dried up" and water lines often are drained away). If you want to find parts in your own body or the body of someone else that need balancing or healing, slowly move the pendulum over the body and scan various body parts: you might find parts where the energy levels are very low (= slow or no pendulum movement). These are usually the areas where you can place your hands and send some balancing energy into the body. Visualise Life Energy from the Stars and the Earth Core flowing through your palms into the body, cleansing, balancing and refueling it with new energies...

Sometimes, high-energy places are Power Places that we can go to when we need to focus or to uplift our energies. Their energy field can, however, be too strong for us to live or sleep there. Cats and ants are, like all animals and plants, good energy readers: they love high-energy places. In the olden days, farmers knew not to build on spots where there were ant hills: they knew that the energy at those places would be too high for humans to live there permanently. They wouldn't be able to rest and sleep.

When to use a pendulum

As said before, people have been using pendulums for a lot of things: for divination, for healing or to find underground water or other resources such as oil or gold. I often use it to test the quality of the food in the supermarket: for example to find out if I should buy certain apples or not. I also use it to check if a medicine or remedy is good for me or not.

If you or someone else in your environment is sick, doesn't sleep well, often feels unwell, you can use the pendulum to check if there are any energies around that affect you or somebody else in a negative way. Water lines, for example, often cause illness and nightmares.

I am sure you will find your own ways when and how to use this Power Tool to detect and read energy fields within and around you.

If you feel energy fields or the answers to your questions already clearly within yourself, you don't need to use a pendulum, of course. A pendulum can be helpful in situations, when you aren't able to read energies clearly, for example when you are distracted by others or need a little assistance ☺

Tips:

1. Keep your pendulum in a nice little bag when you are not using it – to protect it and to honour its specialness.

2. Cleanse the pendulum from time to time to keep its energy pure. You can do this under flowing water (ideally in a natural water source like a river, lake or ocean), by burying it in the Earth (make sure the soil is healthy and not disturbed by pollution, sprays or fertilisers) or in the light of the Full Moon (also see *Cleansing and Clearing*).

3. When I am out and about and forgot my pendulum at home, I use whatever else I can find: the car keys, for example, or my necklace. Be creative and have fun with this easy-to-use and practical Power Tool.

Magic Wand

all ages

Most magicians, witches, wizards, shamans have their magic accessories like wands, drums, crystal balls and other things. Do you need them to create Magic? The short answer is: in most cases NO. However, magic accessories and devices usually support you to focus your energies, to concentrate and to keep your intention. They help to create a supportive setting when entering Magic Realms. A bit like a walking stick: the stick can't make you walk, but it can help you at the beginning to keep your focus and balance. So use whatever magic accessories you fancy, but don't become totally dependent on them.

There is another aspect to this: making Power Pouches, Magic Wands and other things are FUN. While creating them, you weave your energies, intentions, dreams and visions into them – and this will support you on your journey. So magic accessories can be valuable and powerful tools that accompany you on your quest through life.

Magic Wands are staple ingredients of fairy tales, and most wizard and witches have one. They use them to cast a spell. They point their wand towards the sky and conjure up thunder and lightning. Or they transform someone into a stone or a frog or something else. Using a Magic Wand helps them (and you) to direct energy.

Imagine energy coming out of your wand like a laser beam when you direct it towards something or someone. You can use it, for example, to protect people, other animals, objects and spaces by drawing a light circle around them (also see *Protection*).

No matter how you use your Wand: Set your intention well before you use it, and make sure you don't use it when you are angry or frustrated.

Things to consider before you start

Making a Magic Wand or Power Staff can be done in many different ways. The ones I have come across or made myself were made of Wood, Clay or Crystal. Choose whatever natural material you like. Maybe, you just happen to come across a special stick on a walk, or you already have one in your collection of treasures. You can also go for a walk with the special intention of finding your magic companion. Crystal Wands are powerful, but more expensive (you usually need to buy them, unless someone gifts you one). They carry vital and potent energies. Clay Wands are delicate and not so robust, but can be amazing pieces of art if you choose to decorate them.

In the following, I describe how to make a wooden wand. Wood is readily available, comes in many shapes and forms, and can be carved and/or decorated with beads, gemstones, feathers and other natural materials.

1. Choose a stick. Preferably one that has been given freely by the tree = has fallen off and is already lying on the ground. Driftwood is great if you live near a river or ocean.

   If you cut a branch to make a special Wand, please check in carefully with your Self, if this is really necessary. If you feel uneasy or resistance from the tree please don't cut it or find another branch. Always let the plant know what you plan to do *before* you cut it. You can also use Bamboo. Bamboo is a grass and regrows quickly after being cut.

2. Take a bit of time to get to know the stick. This might sound funny, but it is important to get a feeling for the stick and to become familiar with its energy – like getting to know a good friend. This will make your "communication" a lot easier in the future – after all, it is your Magic Wand and you want it to support you in creating Magic.

3. Decorate the stick. You might choose to carve it, do inlays with crystals or gemstones, shells, pebbles, etc. or paint it. You can attach feathers, leather straps, colourful wool – with or without beads. You can wrap embroidered cloth or leather tape around it. The possibilities are infinite! I encourage you to use natural materials as much as possible: because of the pure energies they carry and because you then won't use materials that are processed, don't support life and create waste that won't decompose.

Tip:

Your Magic Wand will reflect your journey and grow with you. You might start slowly and simply and gradually add more and more features to it as you go. Follow your heart and let the Magic unfold.

Playing with Fire

age 5+

I love making bonfires. And I love lighting candles. Watching the flames calms me when I feel restless or upset. I also love the shadow dancers created by flames in the darkness.

Candles spread a special atmosphere, and humans often use them to mark special occasions: on birthday cakes, for a romantic candle light dinner, in church or on graveyards to remember our ancestors.

Here is a simple way to make your own special candles. You can use them for your stillness practice to help you focus: staring into the flame and breathing deeply and steadily will calm you down and help you to relax. You can also place them on your altar or your sacred space, use them for rituals, as gifts or whatever else you imagine.

Self-made candles not only carry your energies, they also don't contain any additives and toxins that pollute the air while burning like many candles you can buy in shops. I use beeswax, because of its purifying and healing qualities (see some interesting beeswax facts at the end of this chapter).

1. Get some beeswax.

   You can collect wax from old beeswax candles or buy beeswax sheets from a local beekeeper, in craft stores or online. There are also sources online that sell beeswax in various other forms for use in cosmetics and for candles.

2. Decide on the shape and size of your candle.

   There are two easy options to make your candle: you can either melt some beeswax (I will lead you through the steps below) and pour it into a container, for example a glass jar, or you can use a beeswax sheet and roll yourself a candle.

3. You will also need a wick.

   I use square braided cotton wick. Hemp wicks are also great. Just make sure that your wicks are 100% organic and not treated. You can sometime get wicks in DIY warehouses or crafts supply shops – or you can order them online. Originally, people simply used twisted fiber strands as wicks. They didn't really burn that well, though: the candles were dripping and the wick had to be cut quite often, as the flame sometimes got too big. The "modern" braided ones work better.

   The size of the wick depends on the size of your candle. The bigger the wick the faster it burns. A general rule is: small candle = small wick, big candle = bigger wick.

   Some suggestions if you use square braided wick:

Candle diameter < 3 cm: wick size #1

Candle diameter < 5 cm: wick size #2

Candle diameter < 6.5 cm: wick size #3

Candle diameter < 8 cm: wick size #4 or #6

Candle diameter < 9 cm: wick size #7

Option 1 – beeswax candle without melting

1. Take a beeswax-sheet and cut it in half.
2. Roll out the wick along the smaller side. Cut a piece the length of the side plus and add three centimeters extra.

If you use square braided wick you will see a "V" in the braid. Make sure the "V" is upright in your candle like the letter "V".

3. Place the wick along one side of the beeswax sheet so that there is an overlap of about three centimeters. Gently press it down with your fingertips so that it sticks to the wax. Then start rolling the sheet tightly around the wick. Make sure that there are no air gaps by moulding the wax with your fingers around the wick.

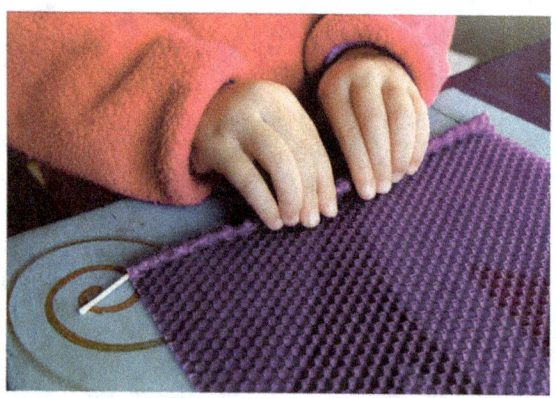

4. Once you have the wick set firmly within the sheet, place your palms on the tiny roll in front of you and gently roll another layer, away from your body. Roll your candle carefully until you reach the end of the sheet. Make sure that there are no big air gaps and that you roll the candle in a straight line to make both ends even.

5. Press the end of the sheet gently to the previous layer to get a neat "seam". Ready!

To make a bigger candle, simply add another sheet: place the second sheet exactly on the first one so that they overlap by about 5-10 millimeters. Press the two sheets together with your fingertips until they stick together nicely. Keep rolling and finish as described above.

Tips:

1. It works best, if you have a clean, smooth, non-sticky surface to work on.

2. Also: Make sure that the temperature is right. If it is too hot (for example in direct sunlight or in summer), the beeswax sheet will start to become soft and sticky, almost melting, and not easy to work with. If too cold, the sheet is inflexible and hard and might break or rip easily when you try to roll it.

I let my beeswax sheets warm up just a little, so that they become flexible and easy to work with – you will find out pretty quickly what works for you and what not.

3. If you break or rip your candle, don't worry: you can always use the beeswax to make another candle by melting it (see option 2 below).

4. You can make different shaped candles: long ones, short ones, thin ones, fat ones, round ones, cone-shaped ones by cutting stripes of different sizes from the beeswax sheet and rolling them together as described above.

5. You can also decorate your candle after you have rolled it. Use leftover beeswax and warm it between your hands, in the sun or another heat source. CAREFUL: beeswax is flammable so don't use direct heat like a gas burner or open fire! Once the beeswax is nice and soft, you can mould various forms and shapes with your fingers, as you would with play dough, and stick them to the candle. Another option is to use cookie cutters and cut out shapes out of the beeswax sheet.

You can also gently press shells, beads, pebbles, etc. into the side of the candle to create patterns and make your candle extra special.

Option 2 – beeswax candle with molten wax

1. Put beeswax pieces into an old (unused) pot, pitcher or an empty clean tin can. You can get old pots from recycling shops. I use empty tin cans and make a dent in the rim with a pair of pliers so that it is easy to pour the molten wax into the candle container later on.

2. Place the tin can with the wax into an old pot filled with water (not too much, otherwise the can will float and won't stay upright). Slowly heat the water over low or medium heat. Important: don't melt your beeswax over high heat as it might ignite. Stir with a clean stick from time to time. I love melting beeswax – the colour is beautiful and the smell is delicious!

3. While the wax is melting, prepare the jars or other containers you wish to use for your candles. I mainly use old glass jars. If you don't have any at home, you can get them from the recycling center or reuse shop.

You could also use tin cans or any other non-flammable containers.

4. Once you have chosen a suitable container, cut a wick at least three centimeters longer than the height of the container you are using. Dip the wick in the molten beeswax leaving about three centimeters at the top uncovered (remember to check the "V" direction if you use square braided wick as described in option 1). Lay it out on newspaper to dry. Straighten it by holding one end with your fingers while gently pulling the other end with a toothpick or skewer. The beeswax will dry quickly and you should end up with a straight stiff wick.

5. Pour some molten wax into the jar, about 1-2 centimeters high. Be careful: the tin can, or whatever you use to melt your beeswax, will be super-hot! You might need pliers or at least baking gloves or a cloth to protect your hands. Stick the (dried) wick into the molten wax in the center of the jar. Make sure the wick goes right down to the bottom of the jar and is straight. Hold it in place for a few minutes until the wax has hardened enough for the wick to stand on its own. Let the wax harden completely – this might take a while, depending on the size of your jar and the outside temperature.

6. Once the wax is completely hardened, reheat the rest of the beeswax and finish pouring hot wax until your jar is filled – leave a bit of space and make sure there

is at least two centimeters of wick uncovered. If you want, you can secure the wick with a toothpick or a skewer, so that it doesn't move when you pour in the wax. Rest the toothpick or skewer on the rim of the jar and carefully wrap the upper end of the wick around it. Make sure that the wick is straight.

7. Let the candle harden for at least a day or two. You can then either leave your candle in the jar or smash the glass, if you prefer ☺ To do this safely and to avoid a big clean-up I normally put the jar in a plastic bag, then carefully tap it with a small hammer or stone until it breaks. Don't smash it too hard as it might damage your candle and potentially yourself! Be careful and avoid touching the glass and the plastic bag with bare hands: sharp glass pieces might pierce through the plastic and cut you.

Interesting facts about beeswax

Honeybees produce beeswax to build honeycomb cells in which their young are raised with honey and pollen from flowers. The wax is formed by the worker-bees who secrete it from glands. At the beginning the new wax is glass-clear and colourless. Over time it becomes a more yellowish or brown tint because of the contact with pollen oils and propolis. Propolis is a sticky mixture that bees produce by mixing saliva and wax with sap or other plant materials.

The bees make little lids with the beeswax to close up the cells of the honeycomb where the honey is stored. Propolis is used as a glue to fill in small gaps and seal off the cells. It takes about one kilogram of lids to cover 45 kilogram of honey. A lot of work for the bees!

***

When burned beeswax produces negative ions that clean the air. These negative ions will attach to positively charged particles in the air such as bacteria, viruses, and allergens like dust and pollen. These so-formed clumps of particles become heavier and "fall" to the ground where they can be swept or vacuumed away. If you suffer form allergies, you can effectively clean the air in your room or house by regularly burning beeswax candles.

I also use them to "clear the atmosphere", for example after a heated discussion or whenever something sad, upsetting or otherwise troubling happened.

Negative ions are also good for your body balance, because they stimulate one of the major glands in the body: the pituitary gland, a pea-sized body part attached to the base of the brain. It is said to control not only your physical growth and development, but also to be the center of creativity, intuition and dream activity. Maybe this is the reason why beeswax candles are often used for ceremonies and Magic work.

***

Beeswax is a 100 % natural fuel, scented by the honey and nectar of flowers packed into honeycombs.

***

You can eat beeswax! I don't know if it does have any health benefits when you eat it – but at least it doesn't do you any harm. So relax if your little brother, sister or cousin swallowed a piece!

***

Beeswax contains vitamin A and is really good for skin and hair. It keeps the moisture in the skin and hair and has anti-allergenic and anti-inflammatory properties. This means it can actually sooth easily irritated skin and help with rashes and other skin problems like eczema. It also heals minor skin cuts, abrasions, scrapes and prevents wounds of getting infected.

I use a mix of organic coconut oil and beeswax (molten together) to protect my skin from the effects of sun, wind, winter cold and weather. If you are re-growing or losing your hair (for example after medical treatment), use a little beeswax to help your hair grow back faster or to stop it from falling out. You can also apply it from time to time to keep your hair healthy, well moisturised and shiny. Use it instead of hair gel or other styling products that usually contain a lot of "nasty chemicals".

***

Beeswax candles normally burn brighter, longer and cleaner than other candles. They emit essentially the same light spectrum as the sun! So you can bring the sun into your home when you are sick, during long periods of rain, in winter, when you are down or in a bad mood – and enjoy the transformation. Let your candles do their magic!

Make your own Smudging Set

all ages

Smudging is an ancient practice to cleanse objects and places with smoke of burning plants, herbs, resins, bark and other natural substances. The word originally means "making a smoky fire". Smudging helps to clear a space or body from negative or unwanted energies. It also supports you to call in your allies from the Spirit World and to direct your intention.

I smudge my house every time after tidying up to clean it not only from dust and dirt, but also on an energetic level. I also do it when I had visitors that brought unsettling energies or after a "heated conversation". If you don't sleep well at night, you might want to try smudging your room and yourself before going to bed. Not sleeping well can also have to do with the location of your bed – let somebody check if there is a water vein under your house. You can also ask your Spirit Helpers, they can tell you, too – or use your pendulum.

Scientists recently confirmed other positive effects of smudging: burning medicinal herbs purifies the air, and the healing substances of the herbs are absorbed more easily by the body. 94 % of the bacteria usually found floating in the air around us (some of them able to cause all sorts of illnesses) are killed by smudging – and not only for a short period of time, but up to a month!

Smudging is a Power Tool that you can use in many ways:

- to cleanse a space, place, object, body
- to disinfect something or somebody
- to protect your Self, others or a space
- to absorb healing and balancing substances into your body
- to lift your spirits (literally) and to help you find balance
- to help you relax and unwind
- to feel more centered
- to call in Spirit Helpers and allies and to direct your intention when doing ceremony or prayer
- to alter or shift your consciousness

You can buy smudging sticks or sets in New Age and health stores, or make your own. It is fun and costs less money – and you will also be able to connect with the plants and choose your own special ones.

I like to use herbs that grow where I live instead of buying imported herbs from a faraway land and culture. Sage, Rosemary, Pine and Lavender are examples for plants that you can find almost everywhere. You can also smudge with bark. In churches people often use Myrrh or Frankincense. Ask around and see what is available for you.

In the following steps, I will show you how to use Sage, Rosemary or Lavender to get you started:

1. Find some Sage, Rosemary or Lavender plants.

   You can easily grow your own in pots or buckets on the veranda, in your room or in the garden, if you have one. Rosemary is easy to grow from cuttings: ask an existing plant if you can cut off a small branch. If you receive a "yes", you can take it and simply stick it in a jar with unpolluted garden soil – it will grow roots and, over time, turn into a wonderful Rosemary bush.

   Once you have sourced a well-established plant (please never take from a young baby plant as it might not survive), cut some branches, about two hand lengths long. Before you cut them, sit with the plant for a while and connect with it. *Feel* if the plant is healthy and ready to share some branches with you. The plant needs to be able to survive, so please only take a few branches. Trust your knowing and treat the plant with respect and care. Thank the plant and invite her Spirit to support and guide you.

2. Dry and bind the branches.

   I let the branches dry for one or two days, but you can also continue with the next step straight away. Cut a piece of thin cord (cotton, hemp or another 100% natural material) about four times the length of your branches. Make a bundle out of a couple of branches, depending on how thick you would like your stick to be. I usually use about 5-7 branches.

   Hold your bundle so that the tips of the branches point downwards and start to wrap the cord tightly around the base of your bundle. Continue wrapping the cord around your bundle towards the tips of the branches. Press the plants together firmly – the tighter they are bound together the better your smudging stick will burn.

   When you reach the tip, work your way back down. Finish off by tying the two ends of the cord together.

3. Let your smudging stick dry in a basket of natural material or by hanging it in a dry airy place, best out of direct sunlight, as the plants would dry too quickly and lose more of their medicinal properties.

How to use your smudging stick

Once your smudging stick is completely dried, you can use it. It usually takes about a week or so. You know it is ready to be used when the leaves are much lighter and, well, dried.

Call in the Spirit of the plant before you light the tip of the stick with a candle or a match. I prefer a candle to light the stick, because it can sometimes take a while until it burns. Once it has a steady flame, gently blow it out. If you are indoors you might want to use a heat-proof bowl or glass to catch any ash from falling down. I use an abalone shell that I found at the beach (see picture above).

You might need to breathe gently onto the stick from time to time to keep it smoking and smouldering. You can also use a feather.

Fan the smoke with a feather or your hand over your body and throughout the space you want to cleanse.

Once you are finished, you can either let your stick burn to spread its Magic until it is burned completely, or you can extinguish it and save it for another occasion.

To extinguish it, put it in a bowl of sand. If you don't have a river or beach nearby, you can get sand from any building supply or pet store.

Treat the ashes with intention: Be aware that you are burning "negative stuff" (bacteria, negative energies, etc.). A safe and easy way to dispose of them is to take them outdoors (if you aren't already) and spread them onto the Earth. If you feel the need, you can also dig a hole and burry them.

A word of precaution: As you are literally playing with Fire here, please be careful and use your senses. I know you will, but I have to write this note of caution, because of some adult rules ;)

If ashes fall on anything flammable (clothes, carpet, furniture, dry grass/twigs, your little sister or brother...) – well, the result might not just be a desired cleanse. So please take care for your own safety and that of others.

There are many traditional ways of using a smudging stick. You can follow those ancient ways or listen deep into your Self and find your own way with this Power Tool.

Here is a basic **Native American way** to inspire you: present the smoke to the Four Directions, beginning in the East where the Sun raises, following the path of the Sun. Greet and call in the Spirits of the Four Directions: East, South, West, North.

Then present the smoke to Father Sun and acknowledge his Life-giving powers. Touch the ground and let the smoke waft across Mother Earth to honour her powers and connect to her energies. You can sing a song or say a prayer to call in more guidance and supportive energies and set the tone for your ceremony.

Begin to cleanse your Self with the smoke, starting on the left side (female) of your body and ending on your right side (male). Give special attention to your heart and head space, both your ears, your third eye (the place between your eyebrows), your fontanelle (on the top of your head; you will feel the spot, it is the place of the skull that is still open when a baby is born and only closes within the first weeks or months of our physical life) and your belly.

Fan smoke all around you and visualise how it takes everything away that doesn't serve you.

Finish the cleanse with a prayer and give thanks to all the Spirit Helpers, especially the Spirit of the plant you are using to smudge.

Extinguish the smudging stick in a bowl of sand or let it smoulder in the background until it goes out by itself. Make sure you dispose of the ashes!

Some Plants and their special powers

- Sage – clearing negative energies
- Pine – cleansing and purifying
- Rosemary – protection
- Lavender – calming and relaxing
- Rose petals – comforting, giving love and support, good for meditation
- Peppermint – healing, protection
- Lemon balm – spiritual cleaning, balancing
- Yarrow – detoxifying

Tips:

1. If you don't use branches but other dried plant parts such as bark, resin, petals, or roots, place them in an inflammable bowl or container before you light them. The container might get hot, so be careful when you hold it in your hand and don't place it on a flammable surface.

2. Some people use small charcoal disks to burn dried herbs, bark, petals and other plant parts that cannot be bundled together easily to form a smudging stick. You can buy them in New Age shops and online. The charcoal smoulders away and burns the dried plant parts. You have to place the disk in an inflammable bowl or container before you light it.

Magic Potions

age 8+

Did you know that a lot of the remedies and drugs that are prescribed by doctors and sold in pharmacies are plant-based? The Plant and Mineral Kingdoms can be our allies, our teachers and healers, if we choose to welcome them into our lives – given that we treat them with respect and care, of course. Sit with them as often as you can and listen...

One way of commingling with their energies is by making Magic Potions. Every thing and every body has its own special energy frequency or vibration. When you make a Magic Potion you can store this special vibration.

Magic Potions are doorways through which you can enter unseen realms. They help you to surf the waves of your life and to transform what wants to be transformed. They can uplift your energies and help you to feel good.

In this chapter I will show you how to make your own Magic Potions. Flowers, plants, gemstones, seaweed, animals, stars, the Elements, dreams – you can collect their vibrations in your Magic Potions and use them to bring balance or protection.

1. Choose a vibration and become familiar with it.

    First, get a feeling for energies you want to link into. Allow your Self to be guided. It might be a weed that is growing abundantly in your garden, or a special flower that you really love. You might want to commingle with Dolphin or Horse energy or bring the power and lightness of the Wind into your life.

Choose *one* energy frequency for your first Magic Potion. Make contact with the flower, tree, animal, Element or whatever it is: sit with it, observe it, feel it, think about it... Connect to it in whatever way you like until you feel that you know it well.

I often allow a long time to connect with the energy before I finally make a Magic Potion. And sometimes it happens that I don't feel the need to make a Potion anymore ;) It is always a good idea to connect with the Spirit of the plant, animal or whatever it is and to become friends with them. It will increase the power of your Magic Potion immensely – and you will make new reliable friends for life!

If you skip this important first step, the door might stay closed and Magic might not flow.

2. Collect Water.

To make your Potion you need water. Water is the Life-blood of our Planet and holds the essence of Life. Always treat Water with great respect. If you can access pure spring water, that is great. If not, use rainwater or, if there isn't anything else, purified tap water. Just use the purest water you can get. Having said this: you can always clear and purify water through the power of your thoughts and intention. Visualise how the water transforms into crystal clear, fresh water. See it in front of your inner eye, *feel* it... (also see chapter *Transfiguration*)

Like talking with a good friend or family member, let the water know why you are gathering it. Ask the Water Spirits for permission to use water for your Magic Potion. If they agree, thank them for their gift. If we treat and respect all life forms like family members and good friends, they, too, will respond openly to us. This is a prerequisite for creating Magic and working together on this Planet.

When you collect the Water, use clean glass jars, glass bottles, a clay bowl or any other container made of natural materials. Plastic affects the energy structure and quality of water.

Make sure the water is free from all debris (strain it through fine gauze if needed).

3. Make your Magic Potion.

Once you are ready and feel that you are connected to the plant, animal, Element or whatever energy you have chosen, you can begin to make your Magic Potion.

Magic Potions can help you when you are stressed-out, ill, upset, sad – in short: they can help you whenever you want to find balance and need some support from the Plant, Animal, Mineral or other Kingdoms.

Below you will find a few different Potions as examples. Be creative, follow your intuition, respect your Self and other life forms – and you will be guided to make many more of your own.

Magic Flower or Plant Potion

You need a small clean glass bottle. You can use recycled ones and sterilise them (see instructions at the end of this chapter). It is best to use coloured glass, so that no light can get in and affect the Potion. If you can't find any, you can also wrap something around the bottle (also see below for how to store your Magic Potions).

1. Choose a flower. Get to know it and tell it what you want to do, in order to open the door for Magic to flow.

2. Once you both feel ready to begin the process, drop Water over the flower *while it is still attached to the plant.* If you pick the flower, it will lose some of its Life-force and can't share its full power.

   You can use an eyedropper or pour water straight from the container. Hold a bowl, cup or glass jar under the flower and catch the water. While you pour water over the flower, ask it to release its Magic into the water and to share its gifts with you and all who will use the Magic Potion.

A word of caution: If you don't know the plant well, make sure that you don't collect water that ran over the leaves or other parts of the plant: they might contain substances that aren't good for you. If you know the plant and its properties (= if you know that it is not poisonous, for example), then this doesn't matter ☺

3. When you have collected enough Magic Potion water, sprinkle a little over the plant as a thank you before you leave.

4. Filter the Magic Potion water through gauze to stop any plant material going into the storage bottle. Otherwise the Potion might go mouldy.

5. I then use an eyedropper to fill half of a small clean glass bottle with filtered Potion water. Fill up the rest of the bottle with organic cider vinegar (you could also use alcohol like Vodka or Brandy). The vinegar will preserve your Magic Potion, so that you can keep it for a long time.

6. Close the bottle tightly. Then hold the bottle in one hand and tap it lightly against the lower palm of your other hand for 21 times, in order to activate the energy. 21 is a magic number that is used in many traditions and indigenous cultures to call in Magic Powers.

7. Et voilà! You now have your own special Magic Potion!

8. If you want, create a nice label so that you know what's in the bottle – especially if you plan to make more Magic Potions over time.

Hold the bottle and sit with it: the Plant Spirit will tell you when and for what to use it. You can also sit with the original Plant, of course. Take only a few drops in a glass of water, as this is a very concentrated and strong mixture. If you want, you can use a pendulum to check how often and how many drops you need to take – or simply follow your intuition.

Tree or Stone Potion

If you need comfort, want to be strong, more confident or want to find balance, Tree and Stone Potions are excellent ways to support you (and others).

In the following I will show you another, easier way of making a Magic Potion.

1. Fill a small clean glass bottle with pure water (see above).

2. Choose a tree or stone and connect with it. Talk to it: let it know *why* you would like to make a Magic Potion. Ask it if it wants to share its energies with you. If you feel its "ok", go ahead with the following steps.

3. Place the bottle between the roots of the tree or wherever it feels right to you. Listen closely, and he or she will let you know where to put it. The same is true when you are working with a stone.

If your tree or stone friend are in an area where other people might pass, make sure that the bottle will not be disturbed: you might want to cover it with leaves or bark or place it inside an opening in the tree or under the stone.

4. Ask the tree or stone to please release their Magic into the water.

5. Leave the bottle in place until you feel it is ready. It might take a couple of days or even longer sometimes – you will know. Trust your Self.

   I left some of my Potions for a couple of months and even years.

6. Follow the steps 5-8, using the method above to make up a Magic Potion. Only difference: You don't have to filter the water, as you didn't pour it over the stone or tree.

Tip:

You can also use this method with any other plant. Simply place the bottle between the leaves or close to the stalk = somewhere within the energy field of the plant.

Crystal Potion

There are very powerful energies held by the Crystalline Kingdom. You can invite Crystal energies by keeping Crystal friends close to you. I have crystals all around my house, most of them on my working desk and next to my bed: they help me write and give me guidance in my dreams.

Here I show you how to make a Crystal Potion. Follow your intuition: you might be drawn to or fascinated by a special crystal. You may love its colour or "special feel". In the *Appendix* you will also find some qualities that people attributed to some Crystals. You might find some inspiration there, too.

To make a Crystal Potion is simple:

1. Choose a crystal, connect with it, ask for its permission to make a Potion and see if it is willing to share its energies.
2. Clean the crystal under flowing water and place it in a sterilised glass bowl or jar. Cover it with pure water.
3. Put the jar in a cool dark place for a couple of days or longer until you feel "it is done".
4. Take the crystal out of the jar and return it to where you found it.
5. Finish the Potion by following steps 5-8 of the first method described above.

Create your Life Potion

This is a powerful Potion to create new directions in your life, to manifest your dreams, to support you with changes...

1. Center your Self. Breathe deeply until you feel calm and strong.
2. Fill a clean glass bottle with pure water.
3. Hold it in both hands, breathe steadily and think of all the things you want to come into your life. Dream it... Imagine it in all details...

   How do you want to feel?

   What do you want to experience?

   What qualities do you want to have?

   How does your environment look like? Your room? Your neighbourhood? Your surroundings?

   What do you want to see in your life?

   Visualise it as vividly and in as much detail as possible. If it is easier for you, close your eyes.
4. Once you see and *feel* it clearly, state aloud what you want to create. Spoken words add power to your thoughts and mind pictures and will help to bring them into your life.
5. When you feel you are done = you have stated all you want to create and manifest, hold your bottle briefly to your "third eye" (the place between your eyebrows). Imagine how all your dreams and visions are transferred into the water.

6. When this process is complete, finish your Magic Potion by following steps 5-8 of the first method described above.

Sterilise your equipment

It is good to sterilise your bottles and eyedroppers in order to clear away all the bacteria and dirt, especially if you are using recycled materials.

1. Put some cloth or a clean tea towel into a big pot.
2. Fill it with clean cold water.
3. Place the bottle(s) and glass parts of the eyedropper (remove any rubber handles or other materials) in the pot. Make sure they are totally covered by water.
4. Bring the water to the boil and boil for about 10 minutes.
5. Use wooden tongs or chopsticks to take the bottle(s) out of the hot water – no metal tools, please. Metal is a powerful material: it interferes with the energy structure and leaves "traces" behind that affect your Magic Potion.
6. Dry the bottle(s) upside down on a clean cloth or tea towel or a dish-drying rack.

How to use your Magic Potions

Take 3-4 drops in a glass of water whenever you feel the need. You can also put 7 drops into a jug full of juice and make your own Magic Potion ice-blocks!

Another method is to rub a few drops directly onto your body. This is especially effective if you do it along the energy centers of your body: on top of your head, between your eyebrows, on your throat, heart, below your belly button and between your legs. My general advice is: center your Self and *feel* where you need it most.

You can also massage a few drops into your soles or palms. A lot of energy lines end in your hands and feet, so if you apply your Magic Potion there, its vibration will have an effect on your whole body.

Add 7 drops to your bath and soak up the magic energy of your Potion. Clear any previous energies with your thoughts *before* you fill the tub: imagine the bath tub being scrubbed and cleansed by a big wash of crystal clear water or light.

You can also use your Potions to support others:

- animals that are in distress or ill – rub the Potion into their fur or put it into their drinking water.
- plants – add 7 drops of your Magic Potion into a watering can or a spray bottle filled with clean fresh water and spray it over your house and garden plants, in the Park, along the road …
- land – you can help the land recover (for example in areas with pollution, de-forestation, building activity) by adding 7 drops to a bucket of water

and sprinkling it onto the land with a small broom or brush.

The possibilities are endless and I am sure you will be guided to use your Magic Potions in your own magic way.

Storing your Magic Potions

Protect your Magic Potions from direct light, heat and other strong energies: wrap them in cloth, preferably natural fibers, and store them in a dark and cool place. If you want, you can keep an amethyst or rose quartz close-by as these stones protect energy fields.

Build your own Medicine Wheel

age 12+

The Medicine Wheel is a thousands of years old Tool to become aware of the unknown and the invisible. I could probably write a whole book just about Medicine Wheels, so this chapter is only a first introduction for you to start your own journey with the magic Power of the Wheel.

Medicine Wheels are used by many indigenous cultures. They help humans to understand how physical, mental (thoughts, beliefs), emotional and spiritual realities all work together. The circle shape represents the interconnectedness of all aspects of Life in general, including the connection with the World of Magic, and your Self in particular.

Medicine Wheels are very versatile, and you can use them in many ways:

- as a compass for your life: your medicine wheel will help you to understand where you are at in your life at certain times and give you guidance.

- as a communication device: to connect with your Self, your surroundings and universal powers.

- As a torch: to help you see and focus on what is within you, in front of you, where you are heading, what you left behind and many other things you need or want to shine some light on.

- as a beacon: to give you pointers, directions and orientation.

Traditionally, a Medicine Wheel consists of the following parts: a center, one or several stone circles and two or more lines of stones radiating out from the center like spokes on a wheel.

Life energy flows in circular and spiral movements. On planet Earth and elsewhere in the Universe, within our body or in our surroundings: we find cycles everywhere. When pure Life Energy transforms into matter, a cell or a physical body develops, grows, dies, decomposes and pure Life Energy is left – until another life cycle starts over again. The Planets in our Solar System follow circular orbits. The journey of water, from the ocean to the clouds and back into the ocean, our breathing, the seasons, day and night... cycles everywhere.

Medicine Wheels are one way to explore these cycles a bit deeper. They make you aware of where you are in a cycle and teach you how to detect cycles within and around you.

There are energy differences between the Northern Hemisphere and the Southern Hemisphere that have an effect on your Medicine Wheel. If you live in the Northern Hemisphere of this planet (for example in Europe, USA, South America, Canada, Russia, Japan), the energy moves clockwise through the Wheel:

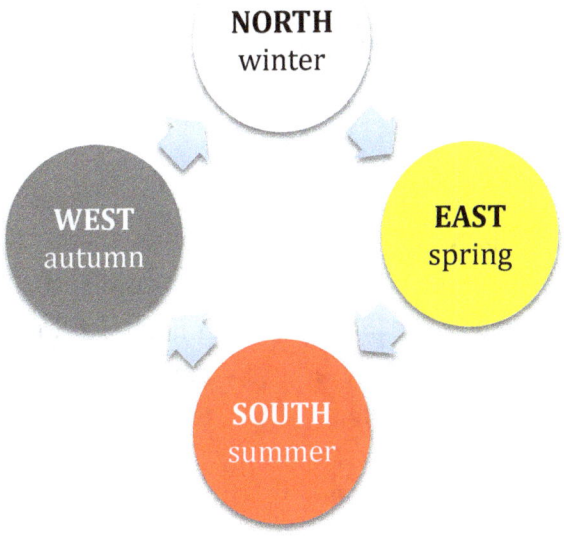

If you live in the Southern Hemisphere (for example in Australia or New Zealand), the energy moves counterclockwise:

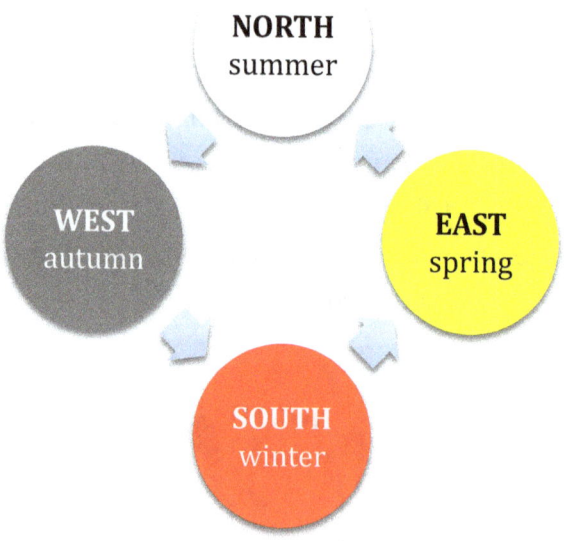

The energies and qualities of North and South are different depending on where you are. In the Northern Hemisphere North is the place of winter, introspection and wisdom. In the Southern Hemisphere South is the home of winter. Simply adjust your Wheel according to your location on the planet.

Examples of how to use Medicine Wheels

The Seasonal Wheel

We all start our journey through life on a certain point of the Seasonal Wheel.

When is your birthday? Babies who are born during the winter season start their journey in the North or in the South, depending on their birthplace. The North (or South if you live in the Southern Hemisphere) is the time to renew and look inside. Spring-born children start their journey in the East with bubbly energy and foresight. Summer-babies come into the world full of trust and innocence. And if your birthday is in Autumn, you carry the energies of thoughtfulness and intuition.

The path of the Medicine Wheel is a path of balance: As you grow older, you travel through all the positions on the Wheel, and you experience different energies and perspectives. It is important to not get stuck in certain positions of the Wheel (for example in your birth position). Keep moving and exploring if you want to find harmony and wholeness.

Play around and see if you can find your current position on the Wheel and the positions of those around you! Sometimes, we jump from one position on the Wheel to another instead of moving from one position to the next (for example straight from East to West). This might cause difficulties and stress, because you might have "missed out" on important learning and experiences when you jump forward too fast. With the help of the Wheel you will be able to understand your Self better – and others, too. It is a good place to replenish your energy levels, gain clarity and get guidance.

The Wheel of Creation

I often use the following basic Wheel when I start something: a project, a new year, a new activity ... It is also helpful whenever I feel stuck in a project, relationship or other areas of my life.

I start in the East:

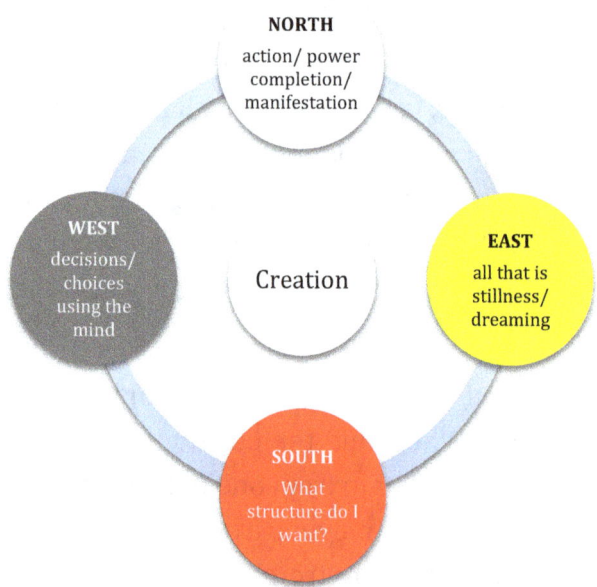

The East: This is the place of infinite possibilities. We are always in an energy field where everything is possible: we are free to dream whatever we want to dream up, no matter what our circumstances are. In order to access this field consciously, we need to become still and calm. If we are focused on what's happening around us or on the constant river of emotions and thoughts inside of us, we are distracted and won't be able to dream.

I usually go down to the river near our house, listen to the constant murmuring of the water and allow my Self to drift off into "Dreamspace". I love this chaotic uncontrolled limitless wild place of dreams, imagination and Magic. I love to enter the unknown and to discover things literally beyond my wildest thoughts. There are no limits like "you can't", "you shouldn't", "you aren't allowed", nothing that is holding me back. I fly freely and explore what comes up.

Some guiding questions here might be: *What do I want to bring into my life? What does my dream life/year /project/relationship feels like?*

The South: Once I got a feeling for what I want to bring into my life – a new friendship, how I want to feel, how my dream life would be like, a new project I want to start –, I move to the South.

In the South I ask: *What do I need in order to make this possible?* I look for a container to hold my dream. Let's say your dream is to be a great football player. Then you would need a field, a ball and some time each day to practise your skills. Maybe you also need or want a coach. Your container holds the energy of your dream and holds a space for it to become true.

Sometimes I realise that the container I have chosen is not suitable: the people I have chosen to work with might not be well aligned with my intentions, and so the project is not taking off as I had imagined it. The container of a relationship, for example, might not bring out the best in myself and the other person, and we might be blocking each other's energies.

An ideal container gives me enough space to unfold my Self, and enough structure to hold the energy of my dream in place. In the case of the football player: the field needs to be big enough to play the game and have fun – for example, a 10 square meter field with 11-a-side definitely wouldn't be fun (or maybe it would). On the other hand: If the field is too big, the players would exhaust themselves, running vast distances.

You can see why finding the right container for your dream is very important. I often realise in hindsight that I need to revisit the South, because I haven't spent enough time in finding the right support structure for my dream. My container might be too tight and not supporting an easy flow. I might have to look for a different environment (location, job, team) to create what I want to create.

Tip:

I learned that all the other steps on my path fall into place very easily and effortlessly, as long as I (re-) connect with the East energy and hold it strong throughout my journey through the Wheel. Some people call this the "power of synchronicity" (= when energies are aligned and work well together to create supportive outcomes).

<u>The West</u>: Once I have found a good support system or made changes and adjustments to an existing one, I can move towards the West. This is the place where the mind kicks in. I come up with plans and concepts to give me concrete steps and guidelines for making decisions. I

write things down to help me keep my focus and clarity about my dream.

This is also the place where sometimes worries, doubts and confusion show up. "Is this really the right thing to do?" "Should I really say no and no longer meet this friend?" "Maybe it's crazy to expect this to work?" If questions like this come up, I re-visit the East again, go into a place of stillness and recall the energy of my original dream. I might also need to check if my container (circumstances) and support systems are suitable. Accept doubts and worries as part of the journey! I welcome them as a sign that it is time to re-connect with the original energy of the dream and focus on what I really want to bring into my life.

<u>The North:</u> This is the place of action and the place of completion. It is where "all things come together" and the dream (project, relationship, etc.) becomes a reality. As long as I keep the East and the South energies flowing, the West and the North usually fall into place quite effortlessly. I often make time in the morning or at night to connect with the East energy –this gives my actions more power and focus.

If I notice that things are "hard and a struggle", that I am pushing stones uphill, I stop and re-visit the East, the South and the West in order to check where things aren't aligned to my dream and my Self.

The Wheel of Creation helps me in many areas of my life: to understand the underlying energies within my Self and others and to consciously align my Self with an effortless and easy flow of energies. I hope it will help you, too.

The Wheel of Balance

Here is another example of a Sacred Wheel that I got from one of my shamanic teachers, Lynn Andrews. It gives you a map to explore the key ideas of balance:

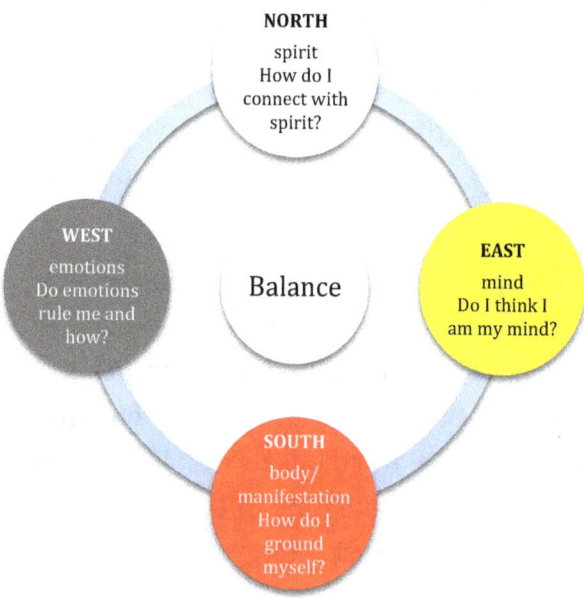

Using this Wheel will help you to deeply understand how you can find balance in your life. Start your journey through the Wheel in the West (Note: normally you enter the Wheel in the East).

The West: Observe your emotions: anger, sadness, happiness, joy, fear, love, hate... *What makes you feel happy? What scares you? What triggers your anger? Do you feel overwhelmed by your emotions? Do they rule you?*

Once you have pondered these questions for a while, take some deep breaths, watch the clouds, listen to the birds, the river or whatever there is around you – and start daydreaming. *What is your "sacred dream"? What do you crave more of?*

Go deep into feeling and dreaming up your dream life...

<u>The North:</u> In the North you explore your connection to Spirit. We are all spiritual beings, no matter if we follow a spiritual practice or not. We can never not be connected to Spirit. When I say "Spirit" I mean the unseen world of universal Life Force. Some call it the Divine Source. Others have other names for it. It is the source from where all Life originates. It is a place to which we best connect with the heart and not with the mind. We can *feel* it rather than think about it. It is the underlying sacred blueprint of everything, the field of infinite pure Life Energy.

Some consciously connect with Spirit through prayer. Others meditate. Some do sweat lodges, ceremonies, rituals. Others dance, sing, write. You can connect with Spirit in many ways.

The question in this position on the Wheel is: *How do you connect with Spirit in your life?*

<u>The East:</u> Your mind is a powerful force in your life. It is like a strong and fast horse that can take you anywhere you want. However, if you don't know how to reign it in, how to give it direction, you might end up lost, in thick jungle, struggling to find an easy path through, clinging on for dear life.

In school you mainly train your mind to become stronger and stronger. You learn to explore concepts and ideas and to think logically. This usually means: you try making sense of other people's findings. In the East you have a chance to explore your mind and how you use it in your life. You can learn to ride this wild horse so that it doesn't lead you astray.

The mind often is highly overrated. We are trained to think, rather than to feel. Here are some interesting questions that you can explore:

1. *Do you think you are your mind?*
2. *When do you act and when do you re-act?*

<u>Note:</u> You act when you are in full control of your action and consciously choose what to do: you ride your horse in the direction where *you* want it to go.

You re-act when your actions are triggered by something that doesn't come from you: for example, something another person has said or done to you, something that reminds you of something that triggers a certain re-action... As a consequence your mind-horse runs off in a certain direction without you taking the reigns, sometimes even without you noticing – and off you go, on a track that you might not even want to be on!

A lot of our actions are actually *re*-actions. If you want to find balance and true inner power it is important to know when you act and when you re-act. Learning to ride this wild powerful mind-horse of yours will enable you to use its strength to your benefit, instead of galloping around randomly and risking to harm yourself and others on the way.

The South: Your journey to find balance through the Wheel will finally take you to the place of physical manifestation: this is the "place of body", the place of dense matter. It is the place where dream energy transforms into "something tangible" = your dream becomes true.

Questions here are: *What makes you feel good in your body? How do you ground your Self?*

The Medicine Wheels that I described above are examples for you to understand the magic of the Wheels. Have fun creating your own!

Build your own Medicine Wheel

Here is an example of how to build your own Medicine Wheel. You can follow it as closely or as loosely as you want. Play around – there is no one way how to it.

1. Find a place where you want to create your Wheel. Outdoors is ideal, because you will feel a closer

connection to Nature in all its forms. The wilder a place is, the stronger the natural balance. You will *feel* the "right place" for your creation.

2. Take some time to connect to the place. Be still for a moment, close your eyes if you want, and greet the Guardian Spirit of the Land and all beings who live there.

3. Wander around "aimlessly" for a while and follow your inner guidance. Take your time.

    You will find four special objects. Your attention will be drawn to these objects without any effort from your side (= you don't have to actively look for them). They will be "given" to you = you don't have to rip them off, pick them, cut them: fallen branches and twigs on the ground, drift wood, shells, stones, feathers, pieces of bone, seedpods, leaves and much more.

    The four objects will represent the Four Directions.

    You might make several trips until you have found your four objects. Take your time and enjoy.

    Acknowledge the Guardians and Spirits of the place, once you found something. Also ask if the objects need or want to be returned at a later stage. If you want, leave something behind as a sign of your gratitude and acknowledgement. Native Americans often use tobacco or corn flour; I sometimes leave grains, seeds or some strands of my hair as a simple gift. Just make sure that it is something natural (= no plastic or chemical stuff).

Another option to mark the Four Directions is to use hand-crafted objects: carved wood or stone figurines, gem stones, images, paintings.

4. Decide how big you want your Medicine Wheel to be. The size also depends on how you want to create the center of the Wheel. The center is the "power point" of your Wheel. Some people even dig a hole in the ground for a fire to mark the middle of the circle. If you want to do this, make sure you have a bucket of water or sand at hand. Winds can arise quickly and unexpectedly, dance with the flames and spread the fire. As Wind Spirits love Medicine Wheel rituals and ceremonies they might be attracted to come and play...

    A Native American chief called Black Elk saw a tree at the center of the Medicine Wheel in one of his visions. You can also mark the center with a beautiful stone, objects that are special and sacred to you, a candle – choose whatever you like and whatever appears appropriate to you!

5. Once you have created your center, place eight stones around it in a circle. Native Americans see the eight stones of the circle as representatives of Father Sun, Mother Earth, the Four Directions, the Powers of Nature and your Self.

Traditionally stones have been used, because they are widely and readily available in many places. You can also use sticks or other natural materials like flowers, leaves, shells to build the circular structure of your Wheel.

6. The next step is to determine the Four Directions. I mainly use my intuition and rarely a compass. Orientate yourself to where the Sun rises in the morning (East) and where it goes down (West). Once you know East and West, you can easily draw the North-South line by making a cross.

    I often sit in the center of the Wheel for a while, before I place the stones and other objects. When I am still and centered (literally), it usually becomes clear to me how to arrange things. Follow your spontaneous impulses. You will know.

7. When you are ready to build your Wheel, begin with the outer circle. First, mark the Four Directions with your four special objects. Traditionally, people place 12 stones along the outer circle line, three on each quarter circle. The 12 stones represent the 12 months in a year's cycle or the three Animal Totems of each direction. Some people also place stones that connect the center and the outer circle, like spokes on a wheel.

    These stone paths were seen as the pathways on which the Spirit Beings and Guardians of the Four Directions could walk through the Wheel.

Before entering the Wheel

When you *feel* that your Wheel is finished, there are a few things that you can do, before you start working with the Magic of the Wheel.

1. As we often carry energies that have an effect on our clarity and openness, it is good to clear our energy field before we enter the Wheel (also see *Cleansing & Clearing Energies*).
2. Be still for a few minutes, enjoy your Wheel, and invite the Spirits of the place, of the Four Directions, your Guardian Spirits, Totems and other supportive energies into your magic circle.
3. Center yourself and set your intention. Focus on what you want to bring into the Wheel. This can be a question, an issue that you want to resolve, or anything else that matters to you in that moment.

Entering the Wheel

In most cases we enter the Wheel from the East, the direction of the rising Sun and of new beginnings.

1. Take a few deep breaths and go to where you are drawn to: *where do you "need" to be?*
2. Once you have found your starting place, sit down or stand still. If it helps you to focus, close your eyes.

   How do you feel?
3. Connect with the Spirits of the place.

Greet them and ask for their assistance.

4. If you come with a special issue, ask the Spirits now to guide you. You might feel drawn to change your position. Follow your impulses and stay for a while in each position where you are guided to be. Breathe and feel and observe what is happening.

   Images might pop up, thoughts, ideas...

   Your Wheel will give you guidance and advice. Over time, you will learn to understand its language and symbols. Use this valuable Tool to connect with supportive energies within and around you whenever you need it.

5. Before you leave the Wheel through the East gate, acknowledge the Spirits and present energies, the Four Directions, Father Sun and Mother Earth for being there and supporting you. You can sing a song, dance, or do whatever feels right to honour the moment.

You can also go on a "**Journey through the Wheel**":

1. Enter the Wheel in the East.

   Greet and honour the Spirits of the East and ask them for assistance.

2. If you have a specific issue, share it now. Be still and listen to answers and guidance. Give your Self plenty of time.

3. Once you feel "complete", move on to the South (Northern Hemisphere) or North (if you live in the Southern Hemisphere). Greet and honour the Spirits of the South (or North) and ask them for assistance. Then be still, breathe and listen to their messages.

4. Once it feels "right" to move on, continue to the West. Greet and honour the Spirits of the West and repeat your quest.

5. Follow the same process in the North (or South, if you live in the Southern Hemisphere of planet Earth).

6. Once you have completed your journey through the Wheel, you might feel drawn to stand or sit in its center for a while. Enjoy the presence of the Spirits and supportive energies around you. Feel their connection to you, and allow them to share their power and magic with you.

7. When you feel ready and complete, move around the Wheel again, giving thanks in each direction and to all energies present.

   Leave the Wheel through the East gate.

Tips:

1. Follow your gut instinct and trust your feelings when finding and placing the objects to build your Medicine Wheel.

2. Take your time when building your Wheel.

3. You can create different Wheels for different purposes.

   Sometimes it might feel appropriate to dismantle the Wheel after you used it. As it is built from natural materials, simply acknowledge the objects, release them and either bring them back to where you found them or spread them in their natural environment. Again: act with respect, *feel* your way through it and follow your gut instincts.

4. There is a lot of information "out there" (in books and online) about the links between different positions in the Wheel and the corresponding energies (colours, animals, elements, etc.). This can be interesting to explore, but be aware that you will find the most accurate information that is directly linked to you and your circumstances within your Self. Be still, be open and listen, and you will receive everything that is important for *you*.

   The more you work with Wheels, the more connected to their energies you will be and the better and clearer you will "hear" their messages.

Weaving Magic

age 5+

In some ways we are all weavers: we weave strands of experiences into a colourful tapestry – our life. Sometimes there might be knots or loose strands or holes, but the whole tapestry is a unique and beautiful piece of art and reflects our path through Life.

Keep weaving your Magic!

Weaving is an old craft and art form that teaches you many things. For example how to be present and focused. Or that many colourful strands *together* make a strong and beautiful tapestry. I am sure you will learn heaps more. Let's get started.

You need: materials that can be used for weaving. Ideally 100 % natural such as wool, strands of plant fiber, cloth (for example old T-Shirts ripped or cut into long strips; you can even tie the strips together – the knots will add a special touch to your weaving), leather strips, stringy bark, fluffy felting or raw wool, dried kelp strands.

As you can see: you can use A LOT OF different materials to weave. And you can use only one type of material or you can mix materials and colours. Be creative!

If you want, you can also add a special touch by weaving in beads, stones, shells, feathers ... Or make "living tapestries" by using flowers, leaves, lichen ... I am sure you will be able to find other things along the way that you might want to weave into your Magic Tapestry.

In the South Pacific people use flax leaves for weaving cloth, cloaks, mats and other things. The Maori people in Aotearoa (New Zealand) call it harakeke.

When you use plant parts that you need to cut off, connect with the plant and tell it what you want to do. Ask for permission to cut a leave. Please be respectful and listen. Don't take anything from the plant if you feel a "no" or if the plant doesn't look strong and healthy. Never take the inner leaves or part of the roots. The inner leaves are the young and most protected parts of the plant: it needs them to continue to grow. You can often recognise the baby or child leaves by their colour: they are usually a bit lighter then the surrounding leaves. Leave a whole leaf family intact to make sure that the plant will live on: parents *and* children!

When cutting the plant, let the plant know *before* you cut it. And please use a sharp knife and make a clean cut.

Thank the plant for its gift.

Method 1 – without a weaving frame

If you weave without a frame, you need rather strong materials. Thin wool, string or plant fibers are easier to use on a frame.

Strands of flax (picture see above), leather, cloth or fluffy raw wool can be woven into beautiful tapestries without a frame. It requires a bit of patience. Be gentle and kind to your Self.

1. Decide how wide you want your tapestry to be. Sort the materials according to their length.

2. Lay out several strands parallel to each other. How many depends on the width of your tapestry.

3. Take one long strip (it has to be at least a couple of centimeters longer than your desired width) and start weaving: over the first strand, under the second, over the third, under the forth and so on.

The first couple of rows can be a bit tricky as the whole structure is still moving. You can use clothes pegs to hold the first line in place, if this makes it easier for you.

Once you finished the first row, you can either weave the second row using the same strand of material (if it is long enough to continue) or you can take another strand and start weaving back to the other side. Weave the strand exactly the opposite way than in the previous row: where you went under before now go over and vice versa.

4. Continue weaving until your tapestry is the size you want it to be.

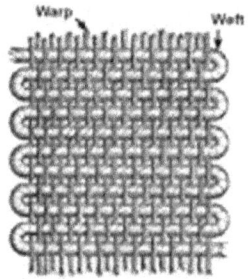

5. Unless you have woven your piece with one gigantic long strip, you will now have a lot of "loose ends" at either side of the tapestry. Take each loose end and weave it into the existing tapestry so that it loops around the last warp.

To finish off trim the bits that are too long and stick out.

Method 2 – with a weaving frame

Some people find it easier to weave with a weaving-frame or loom. Find out what works best for *you*. There are a few simple and cost-effective ways to build a nice loom. I will show you how.

First, you need to decide what kind of materials you want to use and how big you want your tapestry to be. This will determine what kind of weaving frame you need to build.

Square or rectangular looms

Rectangular looms are ideal for you guessed it rectangular pieces. You can build yours out of cardboard or wood. Cardboard is ok, if you plan to use fine, soft materials that are not too bulky.

Option 1

1. Cut a rectangular piece of cardboard the size you need with scissors or a sharp knife.

   Cut notches along both small sides: you need an odd number of notches in order to alternate each row: over, under, over, under.

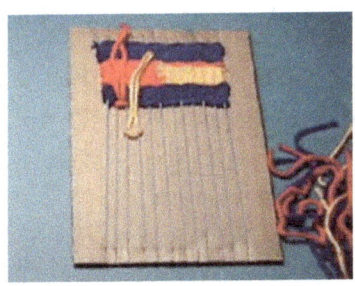

You can choose the size of the cardboard rectangle and the distance between the notches as you like.

2. When you have prepared the cardboard, attach one end of a long piece of strong string, yarn or plant fiber to the back of the cardboard with some tape. Wrap the string from the back through the first notch and all the way to the opposite side of the cardboard, around the back of the notch there, and back to the other side, etc. Continue until you reach the end.

Pull the string through the last notch to the back of the cardboard and attach the end with tape. Now you have a so-called "warp" to weave on. The string, wool or other pieces of material you use to weave your rows is called a "weft".

Option 2

Another easy way to make your own loom is by using four sticks. I use bamboo, but any solid, straight sticks work. You can also use old broomsticks.

1. Lay the sticks on the ground so that they form the shape you want. Tie them together firmly using strong string, yarn, shoe string or leather tape. Make sure that they don't move and wobble while you weave.

2. To make the warp, tie one end of a piece of strong yarn, string or other robust and tear-resistant material to one of the sticks – usually to one of the smaller sides.

Method 2 – with a weaving frame

Some people find it easier to weave with a weaving-frame or loom. Find out what works best for *you*. There are a few simple and cost-effective ways to build a nice loom. I will show you how.

First, you need to decide what kind of materials you want to use and how big you want your tapestry to be. This will determine what kind of weaving frame you need to build.

Square or rectangular looms

Rectangular looms are ideal for you guessed it rectangular pieces. You can build yours out of cardboard or wood. Cardboard is ok, if you plan to use fine, soft materials that are not too bulky.

Option 1

1. Cut a rectangular piece of cardboard the size you need with scissors or a sharp knife.

   Cut notches along both small sides: you need an odd number of notches in order to alternate each row: over, under, over, under.

You can choose the size of the cardboard rectangle and the distance between the notches as you like.

2. When you have prepared the cardboard, attach one end of a long piece of strong string, yarn or plant fiber to the back of the cardboard with some tape. Wrap the string from the back through the first notch and all the way to the opposite side of the cardboard, around the back of the notch there, and back to the other side, etc. Continue until you reach the end.

Pull the string through the last notch to the back of the cardboard and attach the end with tape. Now you have a so-called "warp" to weave on. The string, wool or other pieces of material you use to weave your rows is called a "weft".

Option 2

Another easy way to make your own loom is by using four sticks. I use bamboo, but any solid, straight sticks work. You can also use old broomsticks.

1. Lay the sticks on the ground so that they form the shape you want. Tie them together firmly using strong string, yarn, shoe string or leather tape. Make sure that they don't move and wobble while you weave.

2. To make the warp, tie one end of a piece of strong yarn, string or other robust and tear-resistant material to one of the sticks – usually to one of the smaller sides.

Lead the string to the opposite side, wrap it around the stick, and move it back again. Continue to go back and forth until you have enough warps or until the stick ends ;)

Attach the end of the last warp-string to the stick. Make sure that the string isn't loose. It needs to be tight like the strings on a guitar. Otherwise the whole structure will wobble and move around and make weaving almost impossible.

Option 3

If you like, you can also build a sturdy wooden loom. Scrap pieces of wood or old cupboard doors will do. I am sure you will find heaps of suitable materials at the recycling store. Old picture frames are great, too.

1. Choose the size of your tapestry, find a suitable piece of wood, hammer a row of nails along the two small sides: the smaller the gaps between the nails the finer the end result, but the trickier to weave.

It is important that you have an even number of nails. Tie a piece of string, yarn, etc. to the first nail and lead it to the nail on the opposite side. Wrap it around the nail once, lead it to the next one beside it, wrap it around and lead the string back to the opposite side. Wrap it around the nail next to the first one, lead it back to the next nail on the opposite side and so on. Continue until you reach the end.

When you wrap the string around the nails, make sure it is straight and taut.

Tie the end of the warp-thread to the last nail.

Round looms

If you love round shapes, like me, you can build yourself a round loom and create your own woven mandala rugs, wall hangings, etc. There are various ways to build a round frame: you can bend a thin willow branch into a circle and wrap strong string or leather tape around the ends to hold the hoop together. You can also use the rim of round baking tins (from the recycling store) or an embroidery hoop (from crafts shops). I will show you a few simple options:

1. Draw a circle on a piece of cardboard and a smaller one inside of the first one, about 3-4 centimeters apart. You can use a plate, salad bowl or other round objects as drawing aides.

2. Cut around the outer circle. You should now have a circle-shape with a 3-4 cm rim.

    Cut notches in the rim (see rectangular looms).

    For a big rug you can use a Hula Hoop, or bend an old piece of pipe from the recycling shop into a circle and tape it together.

3. To create the warp on a round loom you can use various materials and methods. I will show you one simple example with a Hula Hoop that you can adapt as you like. It works with smaller circles and other materials in a similar way.

    Use strong string, 2-3 centimeters wide strips of cloth or other tear-resistant materials. Attach the warp somewhere to your round loom. Pull it straight across to the other side of the circle and wrap it around the hoop/pipe/cardboard notch to hold it in place. Make sure it is nice and taut.

    If you have notches (see image below), simply pull the warp through the next notch and straight across again to the other side. If you use a Hula Hoop or pipe, wrap the warp firmly around it a couple of times, moving sideways, before you pull it over to the other side.

Remember: you need an odd number of warps in order to alternate each row of your weft: over, under, over, under... and so on.

Hula Hoop rug

You need:

- a Hula Hoop or an old pipe that you bend into a round shape, then tie the ends together tightly with rope, tape or leather tape
- a couple of old T-Shirts, raw wool, thick knitting wool, leather strips or other rather coarse materials

1. If you use T-Shirts, cut them into long strips, about 2-3 centimeters wide. Experiment with different widths – the wider the strips the thicker and "rougher" your woven piece.

   Attach one end of the material (T-Shirt strip, strong cord or string, leather tape, etc.) to the hoop. Then follow the steps above (see Round Looms) to create your weaving frame.

2. Once you have the warps in place, attach one end of the weft (T-Shirt or cloth strip, raw wool, etc.) to one of the warps right in the center where the warps meet – or as close to the center as possible. Just tie a simple knot (easiest) or sew it onto the warp. Then start weaving the strip up and under each warp-spoke, moving around the circle.

   Make sure the wefts fit snug and tight. You might need to play around a bit: if you push your wefts together too tightly, the whole weave might roll up like a basket once you have cut it off the loom. If it is too loose, your weave might have holes and not hold together very well. Over time you will develop a feeling of how to get a nice result.

3. Continue weaving around the circle until your rug is the size you want it to be. If you want to add another colour or material, you can either tie two pieces of weft material together with a knot. If you don't like knots in your weave, let the ends of both wefts hang

out a couple of centimeters and weave them in at the end to secure them.

4. Once you are finished, you need to cut your rug off the hoop (unless you want to make it a wall hanging – in which case you can also leave your weave on the loom). Stop weaving at least 3 centimeters before you would reach the rim of the loom, so that you have enough space to tie the ends. Cut the warps – one at a time – as close to the rim as possible. Tie the ends together with a double knot.

Once you have done the whole lot, you can either leave the loose ends hanging as a fringe or weave them in on the back of your rug, so that your weave has a tidy and even finish.

Weaving Magic...

Weaving can teach you a lot about yourself.

Look at the colours that you used. Look at the materials. Rough or fine, knotty or smooth and even... The way you weave can teach you how you weave your life...

Can you see how the strong warps hold the whole piece together? What are the warps in your life that hold the many strands of your experiences together?

Your woven piece will always be a reflection of who you are. If you want, you can use weaving as a Tool to explore your Self in more depth. Or you can simply enjoy the meditative and contemplative process of weaving your piece of Magic Life Art.

Tip:

You can use a lot of different materials to weave. Be creative! Experiment! Weave beads, stones, shells, feathers, etc. into your piece. Use kelp, leaves, flowers, lichen ...

Let your Self run free: there are no set rules or restrictions. Play with colours, materials, shapes – and you might find completely new and unique ways of weaving your magic piece.

Show your true colours

all ages

This is a very simple, easy and fun way to explore your Self. Most likely you are already using it in one way or another. If not, this can be a reminder to use it more consciously on your journey through life.

This practical Tool will not only teach you a lot about your Self, it will also help you to feel better when the going gets tough. It is a great navigational device that can support you in surfing the waves while you explore your path through the ocean of Life. I love it, because it is fun, calming and always surprising.

You need:

- coloured pencils, crayons or water colours – lots of different tones and shades to choose from, the more the merrier
- a piece of white paper or card board

1. Spontaneously choose a colour (or multiple colours) that reflects your current mood/feelings/situation.
2. Start drawing...

Don't think about what you will draw. Just let things flow out of you... and watch what happens. You might just doodle and draw random patterns, lines or shapes. Or you might draw a certain form/landscape/animal/object that "pops up" in your mind. Important is that you simply allow the flow to happen and don't interfere with your mind. Don't plan, don't prepare, don't think. Let things come up and have fun with it.

Tips:

1. Choose whatever colours you feel drawn to use.
2. If you feel stuck or uninspired, guide your thoughts back to how you feel – this will give you more "fuel".
3. This Tool is especially powerful when you are upset, frustrated, sad or unsettled in any other way and when emotions and feelings are boiling up. You can also use it when you feel that there is something out of balance, but you are not quite sure what.

It is a great release and revelation Tool that will help you to bring "stuff" to the surface and to get it out of your system.

Dreamspace Art

age 7+

Creating art is an interesting human "thing". Most other animals don't do it to this extent. In many ways, art is magic: it illustrates our magic powers, it links us to the "bigger whole" that goes way beyond our Selves and strengthens our connection to it, it shows us hidden treasures within our Selves and opens our intuition channels. All people are "arty", some more than others. Art can help us to express ourselves and to get in touch with the essence of Life.

There once was a time when people didn't rely so much on the written word. They sat together and told stories around the fire instead. They also painted important messages and information on rocks, teaching survival skills and the use of the land. Most of these images contained symbols representing what people saw in Nature:

MAGIC LIFE ART

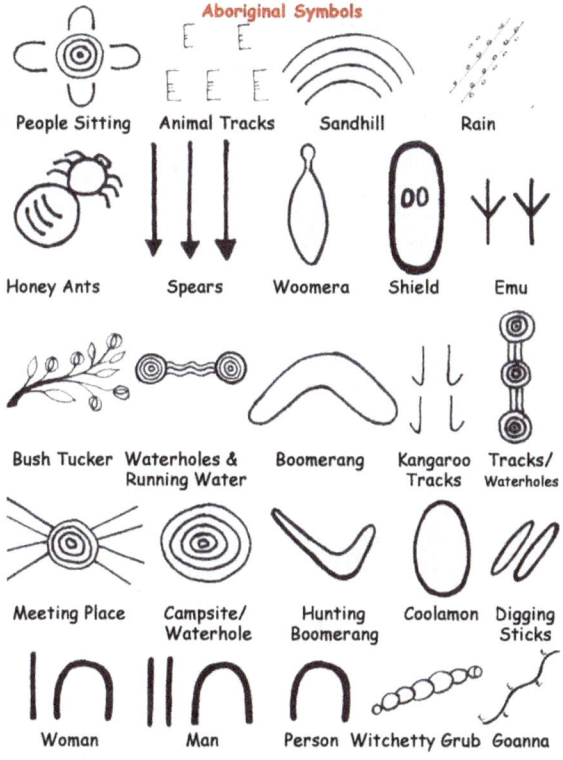

The paintings showed sacred places, important locations (for example water holes, mountains, campsites) and created living maps to help people to navigate through their environment. But they didn't only depict physical things. They also gave advice and guidance about the Spirit or Dreamworld.

If people were ready to read the signs they would be guided to Portals and Magic Power Places, where they could enter Spirit World and connect with other realities. Our myths and legends and books about shape shifters, dragons, heroes and heroines with super powers are remnants of what used to be common and practised knowledge amongst our ancestors.

So be aware: when doing this art, be open and allow things to happen – it might be your gateway to enter a dreamspace that holds valuable information and other treasures for you.

You need:

- lemon juice
- brown-coloured paper, packing paper or cardboard
- paint brush(es)

1. Dip your brush(es) in the lemon juice (use it sparingly) and start painting. Find your own flow and paint what comes up: dots, spirals, circles, lines, ...

2. Let your picture dry, flat on the ground or table or wherever you were painting. Don't move it, otherwise the juice will run all over the paper and create its own patterns – which could be quite nice, too, of course!

Tip:

If you want you can also use this Tool to get advice and guidance from the Spirit World and to find answer(s) to a question: set an intention and ask a question before you start paining and call in your Spirit Helpers. Ask them to speak to you through the painting. Then let it go and "forget about it". Fully immerse yourself in your creation – and see what happens.

Sometimes, the answers or messages take some time to become visible or clear. If you cannot "read" the answer straight away, hang your dried picture somewhere where you can see it – and trust that its message will reveal itself in due time.

Your Act of Power

age 12+

We all bring special talents and qualities into the world. They are unique. No one else holds exactly the same energies!

Always remember this: **you carry unique and special energies that only you can share with the world in this particular way.**

Some people know exactly what they came to share, what they want to do. Others take a while to find out how to best express themselves. It doesn't matter – important is that you always remember that you have special powers.

Special powers come in various forms and shapes. If you aren't sure about yours yet, you can usually detect them by looking at:

- *what you love doing*
- *what interests you*
- *what makes you feel good*
- *qualities you like about your Self*

Some people have physical powers and talents: they are good athletes or builders or gardeners. Others have special mind powers: they love calculating, planning, organising, coding, analysing stuff. There are those who create Magic when they sing, dance, paint, play music, tell stories, make arts and crafts. And those who sit and contemplate and ponder about what Life is all about, why we are here and other questions and then share their insights with the world. Some collect moments of joy and happiness and peace and spread the goodness. Some seek wisdom and truth wherever they go. There are the dreamers who are really good at visualising, imagining and dreaming up things. And people who are good listeners, kind caring friends and advisors. All of us have something unique to share.

Remember: we all need *you* and your unique special powers! Because there is no one just like you. So your powers are important. No matter what your environment might say or think!

You might not feel seen or heard or respected with your special powers in your community, in school, maybe in your personal environment at home and in your neighbourhood. In modern societies, mainly physical and intellectual (mind) powers are acknowledged. However, we need *all* powers for a well-balanced life. If you hold special powers in areas like dreaming, visualising, reflecting, listening, storytelling, collecting thoughts and ideas, it might sometimes seem as if "nobody cares". Or you might feel like you don't really have anything to offer and share that is of value to others around you. Trust me: you have something and it is valuable and needed!

Sooner rather than later your special powers will be in high demand – and if you have been true to your Self and honoured and nurtured them all along, then you will be able to shine your light and literally brighten the darkness around you. You then will become a beacon of light for others to follow. So trust your feelings and tuition from within and follow your heart.

Once you know your special powers – there might be more and more to discover as you grow –, choose a way to express them. Find a form to share them with your Self and the world. How can you make your light visible?

This is what I call your "Act of Power". Imagine that you want to give somebody a drink of water. If you don't have a cup or glass, a lot of the water (= energy) is most likely going to be spilled, seeping through your fingers. If you have a glass, it will help you or somebody else to drink the water more easily and most of it will be contained. Find a container in which you can share your energies, your gifts and make them available to others.

Your special powers can be expressed in many forms. You might want to:
- write a book or a song
- code a game
- compose music
- choreograph a dance
- create a painting, sculpture, carving, collage, etc.

- direct or plan a theatre play, magician show or other performance
- coach others and support them in their learning
- meet with others and discuss "things"
- initiate projects (conservation projects, art projects, social projects, music projects, etc.)
- set up interest groups to share and exchange (school, local community, friends, social media)
- build something (a house/hut, furniture, toys, tools, etc.)
- go on an adventure (a journey, tramping trip into the mountains, overnight camp, solo tramp, river swim, kayak, sailing, riding trip, etc.)
- play with somebody (your siblings, handicapped children, elderly people, etc.)
- make yourself and others laugh or uplift your /their spirits

There are tons of other possibilities. Anything that challenges you to bring your special powers to the forefront, to test your limits and to explore new terrain will provide a good playing field for your Act of Power. Be aware that creating your Act of Power might take time and effort! Sometimes, it might seem easier to give up and not do it. Please stick with it! By all means, have a rest and a break – but come back to it. It will be worth it, and you will be rewarded in many ways. You will get to know your Self better and gain some precious Tools and insights along the way: what do you do when things get tough? Can you persevere and see things through? Or do you shy away? Why? Can you muster your strength to finish a project?

Your Act of Power will bring you a lot of treasures: you will learn to stay true to your Self, to let your light shine no matter what, to persevere and to continue even when things are not easy, when you doubt yourself or others don't acknowledge you for who you are. Most of all: you will learn to fully trust and believe in your Self and your special powers.

USEFUL RESOURCES

Appendix

Trees

Trees are the Guardians of our Earth. They give us the oxygen that we need to survive. They filter the air so that it is clean and healthy to breathe. They are the link between the energies of the Earth and the energies of the Stars. Some cultures call them the children of Mother Earth and Father Sky. They root in the Earth and branch out into the Sky, balancing male (Sky) and female energies (Earth).

They absorb Light energy from the Universes (for example from the Sun) through their branches and leaves, and bring up the Life force and energies of the Earth and the Mineral Kingdom through their roots. In the trunk of a tree, these energies are blended together and create a powerful calming energy field. When you sit with a tree, you can feel this field radiating out to you. This is why trees are such great teachers and support beings when we are out of balance.

The older the tree, the more Life-giving energy and knowledge it has. When a tree is cut down, we not only lose its own powerful energy: as it will no longer blend Earth and universal energies and create an uplifting power field, the land it stood on will also be robbed of essential Life energy and lose vitality.

I encourage you to sit and be with trees as often as you can. Just by being around them you will learn so much! Make friends with them, get to know them and feel their different energies.

Crystals & their healing powers

Crystals belong to the Mineral Kingdom and have been around for eons. They are some of the oldest beings on this Planet and carry a lot of energy and memories of times long gone. Some of them are powerful and wise teachers and healers (also see *Rock Friend* and *Crystal Magic*)

Here are a few outstanding qualities that people attribute to them. I encourage you to find your own ways with them. If you love Stones and Crystals, I am sure they will be your allies and reveal their Magic Powers to you. All you have to do is to sit (or sleep) with them and open up to their messages.

Be patient: it might take a while as they move in much slower cycles than we humans. Once you get used to their way of being, you probably will find it easy to "talk" with them and to receive their messages.

Numbers

Numbers have been used and abused since ancient times. A lot of Magicians, Shamans and wise people believe that numbers have special powers and everything in the Universe can be explained with numbers. From my experience, numbers are yet another way to grasp a glimpse of the whole universal picture. They are another piece in the puzzle and a fun thing to play with. Use whatever comes easy to you to receive fulfillment in your Life and a better understanding of Life matters. This might be numbers – or other things.

Numbers play a big role, for example in Numerology and the Kabbalah (a thousands of years old secret teaching about the laws of the Universe that was only revealed publicly in 1969). If you are drawn to look deeper into the World of Numbers there are many leads to follow and you will find something in a lot of ancient lore, from the Bible to Native American Shamanism.

The Enneagram[7] is another fascinating concept based on numbers that you might want to explore. It is a self-exploration tool that you can use to learn more about your personality. If you like playing with numbers & concepts, you might like it.

Mind reading

Using imagination and visualisation to send and receive messages.

ESP

Opening your senses and linking into other energy fields to exchange information.

USEFUL RESOURCES

Mind Power – Examples

As you have seen in this book, your mind is a powerful tool, especially if you learn when and how to use it wisely. Here some examples of a mind-powered car: https://youtu.be/iDV_62QoHjY, and of a model car controlled by brain waves: https://youtu.be/C7bu26pp2Zs, in case you want to train your mind.

Links

In this section you will find a random collection of links that I found interesting. There are millions of links online, and I am sure you will find the ones that are relevant for you. As anybody can upload anything to the world wide web, use your Power Tools and your intuition to find trustworthy resources ☺

Making shamanic tools, arts & crafts:
http://www.sunflower-health.com/courses/art.htm

Shamanic drumming:
https://youtu.be/WqrBfyCQ0lQ
https://youtu.be/TIwv3eh4Mq4

Clay rattles:
https://www.youtube.com/watch?v=cuY059s5dUs

How rhythm affects our brain:
https://blogs.scientificamerican.com/guest-blog/the-power-of-music-mind-control-by-rhythmic-sound/

Rock and Mineral Kingdom:
http://www.rocksforkid.com/

Effect of words and sounds on water, resonance, everything is energy – with rice experiment at the end:
https://youtu.be/ujQAk9EM3xg

Our universe:
https://youtu.be/rENyyRwxpHo

USEFUL RESOURCES

Enneagram:
https://www.enneagraminstitute.com/how-the-enneagram-system-works/

ESP – Extra Sesnsory Perception:
https://youtu.be/hBl0cwyn5GY

Books

Evelyn C. Rysdyk, *A Spirit Walker's Guide to Shamanic Tools: How to Make and Use Drums, Masks, Rattles, and Other Sacred Implements*

Imelda Almqvist, *Natural Born Shamans: A Spiritual Toolkit For Life, Using shamanism creatively with young people of all ages*

ACKNOWLEDGEMENTS

I want to thank my human and non-human teachers who all shared their special powers and insights so willingly and patiently with me.

Huge thank you to my master teachers, Julie and Noa, my awesome Power Kids. I wasn't always an easy student and often gave you a hard time! I still do... Without you this book wouldn't be here in this form.

Thank you to all the people who mirrored me and encourage me to share and write. Thank you to the many young and old ones who shared their stories with me and allowed me to be part of their journey.

Thank you to my birth family who are always there for me, even though they often don't understand what I am on about and where on Earth I am ;)

Thank you to all the Tree, Plant, Crystal, Ocean, River, Star beings, to my Spirit Guides, to my Animal companions and teachers, to the Land of Aotearoa, the Black Forest region, the Southern Alps and the Pyrenees, the vast forests of Montana, the Mongolian steppe and many other Power Places that have guided and supported me. Thank you to Mother Earth and Father Sky, the Moon and Star energies that keep me aligned to "something bigger" and always make me feel safe and alive.

Thank you, thank you, thank you to all you lovely souls living on this huge and tiny Blue Planet exploring the Magic of Life. Together we are, together we grow, together we weave the tapestry of Life.

ABOUT THE AUTHOR

Birgit loves to dream and to talk to animals, trees and Spirit Beings. She loves to spend time with young and old people and to listen to their wisdom.

Apart from that she writes and publishes books and articles about topics such as Conscious Birth, Interspecies communication, holistic education, sustainable & future gen life styles and shamanism.

Birgit is also active to support women and youth. Amongst other things she holds Red-Tent circles, vision quests (transition rituals) for young women and other courses and ceremonies to nurture female energies and the power of the womb. One of her main intentions is to assist young people to (re)connect with their inner power center and their innate "dream power" to find balance and inner peace and to feel the interconnectedness of all life.

Birgit currently has her "base camp" in Aotearoa, New Zealand. She loves the close connection to nature living in a cottage in the bush.

Find out more:

http://www.moemoea-dreamspace.com/

http://www.power-tools-for-power-kids.com/

http://www.birgitbaader.com/

OTHER TITLES BY BIRGIT BAADER

Books for young readers

Dance into an Inner Light

Balancing and focusing techniques

for children (ages 5-12)

Envisioned as an inspirational and easy-to-follow guide for parents, educators, therapists, and any member of the public interested in sharing valuable centering tools and life skills with young people, this book offers practical examples of how to get started and shows you how to incorporate these effective techniques into your everyday life.

This manual with different meditation and guided imagery techniques will get you started in conscious visualization, a skill that is used widely in many cultures and areas of life around the world. Children are natural masters in visualization. Shamans have used this tool since ancient times to heal, political leaders and businessmen apply it to optimize their desired outcomes and gain insights and guidance beyond conscious thinking. Neuroscience and neurobiology slowly find evidence why these techniques are so efficient and valuable.

No matter if at school, with friends, family, when doing sports, dealing with challenging situations – using these tools will empower your children in many ways and help them to find their center of power and balance and to fulfill their dreams.

Raiti and Moonlight

Moonlight sometimes finds living all alone in a castle very stupid and boring... Until one day, she meets a fairy named Raiti. Suddenly it is one adventure after another.

Will Moonlight be able to get a rare medicine plant from the grumpy Wizard Miraculko's garden to heal her new friend?

Her search for the stitchwort leads Moonlight on an adventurous journey beyond the Seven Hills of Light. On the way, she gets to know not only many extraordinary creatures, but also herself. She learns to trust her path and her duty and discovers how she can deal with life's challenges...

CDs

Dance into an Inner Light

Visualisation exercises & guided imageries

with music

The journeys on this CD support children to find balance and to center themselves, to deal with challenges, emotional and mental imbalances, to concentrate and focus, to self-manage and to gain self-confidence.

All the tracks on this album are using special frequencies and original nature sounds to create a subtle resonance field within the listeners and to lead them further and further into deeper levels of their consciousness.
https://birgitbaader.bandcamp.com/

You will find more details about these and other titles on the website: www.birgitbaader.com

CONNECT WITH BIRGIT

Write me an email:

Dreamspace.moemoea@gmail.com

Visit me on Facebook:

https://www.facebook.com/PowerToolsforPowerKids/

Or visit me on one of my websites:

http://www.moemoea-dreamspace.com/

http://www.power-tools-for-power-kids.com/

http://www.birgitbaader.com/

Interview with Birgit:

https://www.smashwords.com/interview/BirgitBaader

Smashwords profile page:

https://www.smashwords.com/profile/view/BirgitBaader

Endnotes

[1] **Shamanic journeying** is a tool that is widely used by shamans around the world to enter Dreamspace and to access the Spirit World. A shaman is traditionally a person who knows how to travel between the physical and the Spirit World and how to manage energy flow in a life-supportive way. He or she can communicate with other beings, move and shift energies voluntarily (e.g. healing illnesses, shapeshifting, etc.) and alter realities.

[2] **Alchemy** is the medieval forerunner of chemistry; focused on the conversion of base metals into gold and finding a "universal elixir" to give life.

[3] **Sunlight for cleansing**

Be careful: sunlight can be too strong for some rocks, especially if you leave them for a longer period – check in with them *first* and feel how long is ok with them, if at all!

[4] **Telepathy** is controversial in the scientific world = some scientists consider it a hoax as they cannot grasp and verify it with scientific methods. Nowadays, it is used by shamans, in military programs and in parapsychology,

for example. There are experiments and observations that show that a phenomenon like telepathy exists. Babies and children up to the age of 5 show an incredible ability to receive telepathic messages and read people's and animals' minds. You did it all your life and if you want, you can reactivate and refine this potential within you. Make up your own mind (literally) and see how it fits into your world ☺

[5] **Dancing Dervishes**: https://youtu.be/al5ZuZ6_bOI

[6] **Crop circles** – google it and find some initial information here: https://en.wikipedia.org/wiki/Crop_circle

[7] Find more useful information about the **Enneagram** here: https://www.enneagraminstitute.com/how-the-enneagram-system-works/

www.ingramcontent.com/pod-product-compliance
Lightning Source LLC
Chambersburg PA
CBHW071231290426
44108CB00013B/1377